D1558438

The O.J. Simpson Murder Trial

Other titles in Lucent's Crime Scene Investigations series include:

Laboratory Results

The O.J. Simpson Murder Trial

by Craig E. Blohm

LUCENT BOOKS
A part of Gale, Cengage Learning

GALE
CENGAGE Learning™

Detroit • New York • San Francisco • New Haven, Conn • Waterville, Maine • London

LIBRARY OF CONGRESS CATALOGING-IN-PUBLICATION DATA

Blohm, Craig E., 1948–
  The O.J. Simpson murder trial / by Craig E. Blohm.
    p. cm. — (Crime scene investigations)
  Includes bibliographical references and index.
  ISBN 978-1-4205-0038-7 (hardcover)
1. Simpson, O. J. 1947—Trials, litigation, etc. 2. Trials (Murder)—
California—Los Angeles. 3. Criminal investigation—California. 4. Evidence,
Criminal—California. 5. Murder—California—Los Angeles —Investigation
I. Title.
  KF224.S485B58 2009
  345.73'025230979494—dc22
                                                        2008017833

Lucent Books
27500 Drake Rd.
Farmington Hills, MI 48331

ISBN-13: 978-1-4205-0038-7
ISBN-10: 1-4205-0038-4

Printed in the United States of America
1 2 3 4 5 6 7 12 11 10 09 08

Contents

Foreword

The popularity of crime scene and investigative crime shows on television has come as a surprise to many who work in the field. The main surprise is the concept that crime scene analysts are the true crime solvers, when in truth, it takes dozens of people, doing many different jobs, to solve a crime. Often, the crime scene analyst's contribution is a small one. One Minnesota forensic scientist says that the public "has gotten the wrong idea. Because I work in a lab similar to the ones on *CSI*, people seem to think I'm solving crimes left and right—just me and my microscope. They don't believe me when I tell them that it's the investigators that are solving crimes, not me."

Crime scene analysts do have an important role to play, however. Science has rapidly added a whole new dimension to gathering and assessing evidence. Modern crime labs can match a hair of a murder suspect to one found on a murder victim, for example, or recover a latent fingerprint from a threatening letter, or use a powerful microscope to match tool marks made during the wiring of an explosive device to a tool in a suspect's possession.

Probably the most exciting of the forensic scientist's tools is DNA analysis. DNA can be found in just one drop of blood, a dribble of saliva on a toothbrush, or even the residue from a fingerprint. Some DNA analysis techniques enable scientists to tell with certainty, for example, whether a drop of blood on a suspect's shirt is that of a murder victim.

While these exciting techniques are now an essential part of many investigations, they cannot solve crimes alone. "DNA doesn't come with a name and address on it," says the Minnesota forensic scientist. "It's great if you have someone in custody to match the sample to, but otherwise, it doesn't help. That's the investigator's job. We can have all the great DNA evidence in the world, and without a suspect, it will just sit on the shelf. We've all seen cases with very little forensic evidence get solved by the resourcefulness of a detective."

While forensic specialists get the most media attention today, the work of detectives still forms the core of most criminal investigations. Their job, in many ways, has changed little over the years. Most cases are still solved through the persistence and determination of a criminal detective whose work may be anything but glamorous. Many cases require routine, even mind-numbing tasks. After the July 2005 bombings in London, for example, police officers sat in front of video players watching thousands of hours of closed-circuit television tape from security cameras throughout the city, and as a result were able to get the first images of the bombers.

The Lucent Books Crime Scene Investigations series explores the variety of ways crimes are solved. Titles cover particular crimes such as murder, specific cases such as the killing of three civil rights workers in Mississippi, or the role specialists such as medical examiners play in solving crimes. Each title in the series demonstrates the ways a crime may be solved, from the various applications of forensic science and technology to the reasoning of investigators. Sidebars examine both the limits and possibilities of the new technologies and present crime statistics, career information, and step-by-step explanations of scientific and legal processes.

The Crime Scene Investigations series strives to be both informative and realistic about how members of law enforcement —criminal investigators, forensic scientists, and others—solve crimes, for it is essential that student researchers understand that crime solving is rarely quick or easy. Many factors—from a detective's dogged pursuit of one tenuous lead to a suspect's careless mistakes to sheer luck to complex calculations computed in the lab—are all part of crime solving today.

O.J. and Nicole: Trouble in Paradise

Customers could hardly miss the young waitress who carried drinks across the brick patio of a trendy Beverly Hills club called the Daisy. She looked like the ideal California girl: blond and beautiful, with a deep tan and a trim, athletic body. Born in Frankfurt, Germany, Nicole Brown was raised in Southern California, the second of four daughters born to Juditha and Louis "Lou" Brown. As a child, Nicole was headstrong and something of a troublemaker, often getting into mischief with her older sister, Denise. As she grew into an attractive and popular adolescent, Nicole quite naturally became homecoming queen at Dana Hills High School. She took the waitress job at the Daisy just a few weeks after her graduation. Although Nicole was still just a teenager, her good looks and outgoing personality drew admiring glances from the Daisy's male customers.

One customer in particular had eyes for Nicole Brown in the early summer of 1977. After being introduced to her one day, he returned on the following days to see her, to chat, and to flirt with her. "It was instant infatuation," a friend later recalled. "[He] was very attracted to her. It was clear."[1] What was also clear to anyone watching was the age difference between the two: She was eighteen, he was thirty. But if people stared, it did not matter to the man who had become so attracted to Brown. O.J. Simpson was used to having all eyes focused on him.

Orenthal James "O.J." Simpson was born in San Francisco and grew up in a lower-middle-class neighborhood, the third of James and Eunice Simpson's four children. From about the age of two Orenthal suffered from rickets, a disease brought on by inadequate nutrition. The disorder caused his legs to be weak and skinny, and he was forced to wear heavy homemade braces to compensate for the condition.

Simpson's frail body eventually grew strong, and he became a star athlete. As a running back at the University of Southern California, Simpson won the coveted Heisman Trophy in 1968, an honor given annually to the most outstanding college football player. When he turned pro and signed with the Buffalo Bills, he became the first player to rush for more than 2,000 yards (1,829m) in a single season. Injuries prematurely ended his football career in 1979, so Simpson turned to

O.J. Simpson accepts the prestigious Heisman Trophy for college football in 1968. Simpson became a well-known celebrity, first through football, and later through his acting career.

Hollywood, where he remained in the public eye by appearing in movies and television shows. He also was a commentator for *Monday Night Football* and a spokesman for Hertz Rent-A-Car, where his football days were recalled in television commercials featuring Simpson running through airports. Simpson's friendly disposition and natural charm made him a well-liked and much admired—not to mention wealthy—public figure. If Simpson had a dark side, most people on the street did not know it. To them he was simply O.J., "the Juice," the All-American athlete with the warm smile and glamorous lifestyle.

Simpson and Brown began dating in the summer of 1977. At the time, Simpson was still married to his first wife, Marguerite. It was a troubled marriage, with Marguerite often left alone while Simpson traveled for football or on business trips. Marguerite and Simpson separated in 1978 and divorced the next year. Shortly after the Simpsons' divorce, Brown moved into Simpson's mansion on Rockingham Avenue in the affluent Brentwood district of West Los Angeles. They waited seven more years before getting married, the ceremony taking place on February 2, 1985. They eventually had two children: a daughter, Sydney, and a son, Justin. Despite their glamorous lifestyle, their marriage was tumultuous. Numerous violent incidents occurred between 1986 and 1989, and police were repeatedly brought out to their home to investigate O.J. physically abusing Nicole, throwing her against walls and pushing her from a moving car. Photographs taken in 1989 show a bruised and battered Nicole after a New Year's Eve party. By 1992 O.J. and Nicole were divorced. But even though their marriage had ended, their relationship did not. O.J. at times tried to reconcile with Nicole, and he displayed jealousy about her seeing other men.

On the night of October 25, 1993, a Los Angeles 911 operator received a frantic call for help. "My ex-husband has just broken into my house and he's ranting and raving outside in the front yard." The operator asked, "What does he look like?"

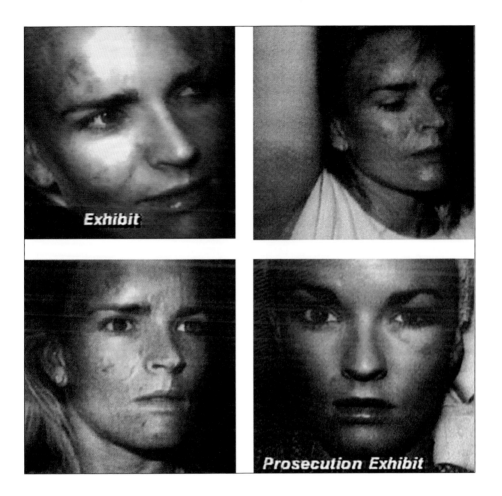

The caller replied: "He's O.J. Simpson. I think you know his record."[2] A sobbing Nicole Simpson said that O.J. had broken down the back door of her house and was threatening her. The operator could hear O.J. angrily yelling in the background. Once the police arrived, the confrontation ended without incident. On another occasion, Nicole told her mother that O.J. was stalking her. "I'm scared," she said. "I go to the gas station, he's there. I go to the Payless Shoe Store, and he's there. I'm driving, and he's behind me."[3] On the night of June 12, 1994, Nicole Simpson and her friend, Ronald Lyle Goldman, were brutally murdered outside Nicole's home. Did O.J. Simpson's obsession with his ex-wife turn ultimately to murder?

These photos feature a bruised and battered Nicole Brown Simpson. She maintained that O.J. Simpson was abusive during their marriage and afterward.

Ron Goldman, shown here in a 1991 photo, was the second murder victim found by Los Angeles police at Nicole Simpson's residence.

The O.J. Simpson murder trial, sometimes referred to as "the Trial of the Century," was held to determine the answer to that question. Simpson was the first, and only, suspect in the case. Forensic science played a major role in the prosecution's attempt to prove that Simpson was, in fact, the murderer. During the eight-month trial, more than eight hundred pieces of evidence were exhibited to the members of the jury, who had to sit through complicated and often tedious explanations of what the prosecution was showing them. When there are no eyewitnesses to a crime, forensic science often supplies the only evidence available to convince a jury of a defendant's guilt. The O.J. Simpson murder trial hinged on such evidence, particularly blood found at the crime scene and at other locations. But such evidence is not always foolproof. Specific procedures must be followed when collecting forensic evidence, and the samples must be properly handled and stored in order for them to be useful in court. Any departure from correct forensic practice may create a "reasonable doubt" in the minds of the jury; this doubt is all that is necessary for the defendant to receive a verdict of "not guilty." The way that forensic evidence was handled became a key point in the Simpson murder trial, one of the most publicized and controversial trials in American legal history.

CHAPTER 1

Murder on Bundy Drive

Sunday, June 12, 1994, was to be a happy day for Nicole Simpson. At 4:30 that afternoon Simpson's nine-year-old daughter, Sydney, was appearing in a dance recital at her school, the Paul Revere Middle School in Brentwood. The whole family was there: Simpson; her mother and father, Lou and Juditha Brown; her sisters Denise and Dominique; and three cousins. The group was already seated when Sydney's father, O.J. Simpson, arrived. He waved to the Browns, then came over and said a few words to Denise and her parents. He said nothing to Nicole, who had not wanted him there in the first place. According to Denise, there was something about O.J.'s demeanor that frightened her. "He just had a very different look about him," she recalls. "It was more of a . . . glazed over [look], kind of frightening, dark eyes. It just didn't look like the O.J. we knew."[4] O.J. spent most of the recital sitting at the back of the crowded auditorium, staring at Nicole.

When the two-hour recital ended, the auditorium quickly emptied. Families lingered in the parking lot in the late afternoon sun, taking pictures and chatting with friends. The Browns had made a reservation at Mezzaluna, a popular local restaurant, for a post-recital celebration dinner. O.J. Simpson was also standing outside, talking to various members of the Brown family. As they prepared to leave for the restaurant, O.J. asked if he could join them. Nicole's answer was a resounding no. She was tired of her ex-husband's obsession with her and had finally put behind her any thoughts of reconciliation.

The dinner at Mezzaluna was a pleasant affair, with everyone in good spirits, laughing and discussing plans for future vacation trips with the children. At some point during

Nicole Simpson and her family had dinner at Mezzaluna restaurant to celebrate her daughter's dance recital. Ron Goldman, a friend of Nicole's, was a waiter there.

the evening, Nicole Simpson noticed that one of the waiters there was a young man with whom she was acquainted. Although he was not serving their table that night, Ronald Lyle "Ron" Goldman stopped by to say hello to Simpson. Like many young people in Los Angeles, the handsome twenty-five-year-old supported himself waiting tables and modeling part time until success came along. For many, that success meant acting; but for Ron Goldman, it was opening his own restaurant. Although Simpson and Goldman went to dance clubs and had an occasional dinner together, they were not romantically involved. She introduced him to her family, and the party continued while Goldman went back to work.

By about 8:30 P.M. the dinner was over and the family left the restaurant, lingering outside in the waning daylight to say their good-byes. At some point during the evening, Juditha Brown had dropped her glasses outside of Mezzaluna. She thought she might have left them in her car, but a search did not turn them up. As the Browns drove off, Juditha decided she would call the restaurant when she arrived home.

As a special treat to end the day, Nicole Simpson took Sydney and Justin to an ice cream shop across the street. Afterward, they jumped into her Jeep Cherokee and drove home. When they finally reached her condominium at 875 South Bundy Drive, Simpson put the children to bed in their upstairs bedrooms. At about 9:40 Simpson's phone rang. It was her mother, who explained that a Mezzaluna employee had found her lost glasses on the curb outside the restaurant. Would Simpson pick them up for her tomorrow? Simpson said she would take care of it and immediately called Mezzaluna, asking to speak to Ron Goldman. Simpson asked Goldman if he would bring the glasses over to her house, and he agreed to drop them off on his way to meet some friends for a drink. At 9:50 Goldman left the restaurant, carrying Juditha Brown's glasses in a white business envelope that had the words "Prescription glasses. Nicole Simpson will pick up" written on it.

Simpson put some soft music on the stereo and began lighting candles in the living room. She also filled her bathtub and placed more candles along the rim of the tub. Was she preparing for a romantic encounter? Or was she simply planning to take a relaxing bath and retire early? No one knows what Simpson had in mind on this, the last night of her life.

A Plaintive Wail

A few blocks away from Nicole Simpson's condominium, Steven Schwab was walking his dog as he usually did around the same time every night after watching a favorite television show. He strolled along his regular route when, at 10:55 P.M., he saw a large white dog standing alone in a dark alley behind South Bundy Drive. The dog, which he recognized as an Akita, was acting strangely, barking at one of the houses along the alley for a few minutes, stopping, and then starting to bark again. Other neighbors had also heard the dog, one describing the sound as the "plaintive wail of a distressed animal."[5]

Schwab approached the dog and saw that he was wearing a collar but no identification tags. Then he noticed that there was blood on the dog's paws, legs, and chest. Finding no wounds on the dog, and thinking it would return to its home, Schwab continued his walk. But the dog followed him back to his apartment, continuing to bark and wail at houses they passed.

By the Numbers

33%

The percentage of female murder victims killed by a spouse or boyfriend.

When he arrived home, Schwab encountered Sukru Boztepe, a neighbor who lived in the apartment downstairs. Boztepe volunteered to take the dog for the night. But the Akita became nervous and agitated in Boztepe's apartment, so he and his wife decided to take it for a walk, hoping to find its owners. They put a leash on the animal and then set out into the night. The dog seemed to know where it wanted to go, pulling Boztepe through the dark neighborhood. Suddenly, the Akita stopped in front of 875 South Bundy Drive, his attention fixed on the darkened walkway leading to the condominium. When Boztepe saw what the dog was looking at, he was horrified. "I saw a lady lying down full of blood,"[6] he later recalled. Boztepe and his wife ran across the street and knocked on the door of a house, telling the occupant to call 911. About five minutes later, at 12:13 A.M., the first Los Angeles Police Department (LAPD) officers arrived at the scene.

Boztepe led Officer Robert Riske and his partner, Officer Miguel Terrazas, to the tiled walkway at 875 Bundy. Riske's service flashlight revealed the body of a blond woman slumped

on the ground at the far end of the walkway, at the bottom of a short flight of stairs. She wore a black dress and was covered in blood, as was the walkway leading up to the body. In the blood, Riske noticed paw prints made by a dog. Riske and Terrazas approached the body, being careful not to step on the bloody walkway. In a landscaped area a few feet off the walkway the officers discovered the body of a man, also covered in blood. A brief visual inspection of the victims confirmed that they were dead.

The two officers called for backup and then began to survey the crime scene. They noticed that the home's front

Yellow police tape cordons off Nicole Simpson's home, now a double-murder crime scene, on Bundy Drive on June 13, 1994.

A Los Angeles police detective points to a bloody left-hand glove found at the Bundy Drive crime scene.

door was standing open, although there was no evidence of forced entry. They cautiously entered the condominium and looked around. There was no sign of any other victims or any blood on the carpeting. The place had not been ransacked, as it might have been if the murders were part of a burglary. Upstairs the officers found two children sleeping in separate bedrooms. Mercifully, they had slept through the brutal crime that had taken place outside their home.

Back downstairs, Riske inspected the living room. He found photographs picturing O.J. Simpson with a blond woman and other family members. He also noticed an envelope bearing Simpson's return address. He concluded that the female victim was likely Simpson's ex-wife, and he realized that any crime that might involve a celebrity would be big news. Since reporters regularly monitor police radio frequencies, Riske used the telephone in the kitchen to call his supervisor, Sergeant David Rossi, to request additional backup and inform him that this might turn into a high-profile case. At this point, no one had any idea of just how high profile it would become.

At the Scene

Soon more than a dozen uniformed officers were milling around the residence, which was cordoned off by yellow police tape. These patrol officers were there only to make sure the area was secure. They knew the golden rule of crime scene management: "Never touch, change, or alter anything until identified, measured and photographed."[7] The actual investigation was left to detectives, criminalists, and evidence technicians. Homicide detective Mark Fuhrman and his supervisor, Ronald Phillips, were the first detectives to arrive, checking in at 2:10 A.M. Fuhrman, at this point the lead investigator on the case, began taking notes on his observations as he walked around the crime scene. He noted several items lying near the bodies. Among these were a white bloodstained envelope, a dark-colored knit cap (which Fuhrman mistakenly thought was a ski mask), a takeout restaurant menu, and a single bloody left-hand glove. Back inside the house, Fuhrman was finishing his notes when he was told that the case was going to be assigned to the elite Robbery/Homicide Division (RHD). This crack investigative section could assemble the considerable manpower necessary for such a high-profile case.

Detective Philip Vannatter of the RHD arrived at the crime scene at 4:05 A.M., followed twenty minutes later by his partner, Tom Lange. By the time Lange arrived, Detective Phillips had already shown Vannatter the crime scene. When Lange viewed the bodies, he told his partner, "This is a classic overkill. This isn't just some robbery, then a cut and run. . . . Phil, this is a rage killing."[8] Vannatter obtained Fuhrman's notes and placed a call to the county coroner to be ready to come to the crime scene when the detectives were through investigating.

An order had come down from an LAPD commander that O.J. Simpson should be informed in person of his ex-wife's death. Simpson also would have to be advised that his children had been taken to the West Los Angeles police station and that he had to pick them up. Vannatter decided that he and the three other detectives—Lange, Phillips, and Fuhrman—would go to Simpson's house and notify the former football star. Taking two cars, the investigators drove the two miles to Simpson's gated estate at Rockingham Avenue and Ashford Street.

Over the Wall

Arriving at the mansion at around 5:00 A.M., the first thing Vannatter noticed was a car parked on the street in front of the house: a white 1994 Ford Bronco. The detectives went to the mansion's Ashford Street gate and rang the bell for fifteen minutes, but they received no response. This seemed strange to Vannatter since he could see lights on inside the house and had been told that Simpson had a live-in maid. After obtaining Simpson's telephone number from the company that provided security for the estate, Phillips called the house. The detectives could hear the phone ringing inside and then the answering machine picking up.

While the others were trying to contact the estate's occupants, Fuhrman walked back to where the Bronco was parked. He noticed a spot of what appeared to be blood just above the driver's side door handle as well as other spots at the bottom of the door. A quick license plate check showed the Bronco was registered to the Hertz Corporation—the company for which Simpson was a spokesman. Fuhrman called the other detectives over to the Bronco and showed them the spots. "Something's wrong," Lange said. "Lights on. Cars everywhere. No one's answering. What if Simpson and his maid are in trouble in there?"[9] At 5:30 Vannatter called for a criminalist

Encountering O.J. Simpson

When police found O.J. Simpson's white Ford Bronco parked at his estate with blood spots on it, they concluded that Simpson had used the vehicle to drive to and from the crime scene. But had anyone actually seen Simpson driving the Bronco that night? One person came forward to say that she had.

Jill Shively lived about 1 mile (1.6km) from Nicole Simpson's Brentwood condominium. On June 12, 1994, she decided to go to a local salad bar. Shively was in a hurry, trying to beat the store's 11:00 P.M. closing time. At about 10:50, as she approached an intersection, she was nearly hit by a white Bronco. Slamming on their brakes, Shively and the other vehicle came to a stop. A gray Nissan also screeched to a halt, blocking the Bronco. The driver of the Bronco leaned out and began yelling at the Nissan's driver to move his car. Shively recognized the Bronco's driver: It was O.J. Simpson.

Although Shively would have made a key witness for the prosecution, she was never called to testify. She had received five thousand dollars for telling her story to the tabloid television show *Hard Copy*, a move that called her credibility into question.

to be dispatched to the Simpson mansion. Then he made a difficult decision: They would have to enter the estate without a search warrant to determine if everything was all right. As the most junior officer at the scene (as well as the youngest and fittest), Fuhrman volunteered to scale the 5 foot (1.5m) stone wall, which he did with little difficulty. Once he was on the other side, Fuhrman unlatched the gate and the four detectives walked up the driveway toward the mansion.

At the entrance to the home they repeatedly rang the doorbell and knocked on the door. Receiving no response, they decided to go to the rear of the house. Behind the mansion were a swimming pool, a tennis court, and a row of small bungalows attached to the main house. Knocking on the door of one of the bungalows, the detectives roused the occupant from his bed. Brian "Kato" Kaelin, a live-in houseguest at the Simpson residence, opened the door, still groggy from sleep. When asked where Simpson was, Kaelin said that he did not know.

Kato Kaelin's Story

Kaelin, a blond would-be actor with the looks and manner of a Southern California surfer, said that Simpson had been at the estate earlier that evening. Around 9:10 P.M. Kaelin and Simpson left Rockingham in Simpson's Bentley automobile to get something to eat. They rode mostly in silence; according to Kaelin, Simpson seemed preoccupied. Driving to a nearby McDonald's restaurant, they ordered food in the drive-thru lane. After handing Kaelin his order, Simpson quickly ate his food in the car. At the estate, Kaelin went back to his room to eat while Simpson remained outside by the car. After finishing his meal, Kaelin sat on his bed watching television and making phone calls. Some time later, Kaelin experienced something strange. As Fuhrman later recalled, "Kaelin told me [that] at about 10:45 P.M., he heard and felt a couple of loud thumps on the wall above his bed. He thought there had been an earthquake, because the thumps had caused the picture above his bed and to the right of the air conditioner to shake."[10]

Kaelin grabbed a small flashlight and went outside to see if he could find the cause of the noises. As he walked around the house, he noticed a white limousine outside the Ashford Avenue gate. He knew that Simpson was taking a late-night flight to Chicago for a Hertz corporate meeting the next day, and he concluded that this was the limousine that would take him to the airport.

For the past several minutes, limousine driver Allan Park had been ringing the intercom buzzer to be let into the es-

tate. Since no one answered his rings, he called his boss to see if perhaps Simpson was running late. While he was on the phone, Park noticed Kaelin walking toward the rear of the bungalows, flashlight in hand. A few moments later, Park saw a shadowy figure in dark clothes walking toward the entrance to the mansion. Park later described the person as an African American, 6 feet (1.8m) tall and weighing about 200 pounds (90.7kg). Soon Park noticed lights come on in the mansion. He buzzed the intercom again, and this time Simpson immediately replied that he would be out in a minute.

At O.J. Simpson's trial, limousine driver Allan Park demonstrates to the jury how he frequently checked his watch while waiting for Simpson to appear the night of June 12.

Processing a Crime Scene

Proper processing of a crime scene by crime scene investigators ensures that important evidence will not be overlooked or accidentally destroyed.

1 Interview the first officers on the scene (or the victim) to determine, in general, what crime was committed and when and how it was carried out.

2 Examine the crime scene to try to corroborate what was learned in the interview. Get a general layout of the scene, and begin looking for possible evidence.

3 Photograph the crime scene. Take wide-angle shots to create a record of what the scene looks like, and take close-ups of evidence.

4 Make a sketch to establish the layout of the scene, the positions of homicide victims, and the relative location of evidence to other objects in the scene.

5 Process the crime scene. Identify and collect physical evidence for laboratory analysis.

Meanwhile, Kaelin walked around to the back of the guest bungalows, where there was a narrow pathway between the bungalows and the property's fence. When he reached the path, Kaelin hesitated. What if whoever made the noises was still back there? Thinking better of his plan, he headed back toward the front of the estate, noticing that the limousine was still outside the gate. He went to the control box and pushed the button that opened the gate. Park pulled the car up the driveway and stopped at the front door of the house.

When Park got out, Kaelin introduced himself and asked if Park had heard anything about an earthquake. Park said no. While Park waited at the front door, Kaelin went back to the dark pathway to take another look. Again, he ventured only a short distance down the path when his unease once more told him to retreat. Returning to the front of the house, Kaelin now saw Simpson standing with Park by the limousine. As he walked back up the driveway, Kaelin noticed a blue duffle bag on the ground. Afraid Simpson might forget to take the bag,

Kaelin called out that he would bring it to Simpson. "No, no, I'll get it,"[11] Simpson replied, walking all the way over to where Kaelin stood to grab the bag.

When Kaelin told Simpson about the noises behind his room, Simpson offered to find a better flashlight and help look for the cause. But when he glanced at the kitchen clock and realized it was 11:15, Simpson said he had to leave now or miss his flight. After instructing Kaelin to turn on the estate's alarm system, Simpson left for the airport in the white limousine, flashing Kaelin a thumbs-up sign through the window.

The Bloody Glove

While Kaelin was telling his story to Vannatter, Fuhrman decided to go behind the bungalows to see if he could discover

The infamous bloody glove was photographed where it was found at Simpson's Rockingham Avenue residence by Detective Mark Fuhrman.

what might have made the noises. Walking along a narrow pathway between the rear of the bungalows and a chain-link fence that marked the boundary of the property, Fuhrman swept his flashlight beam around. He soon approached the point where he estimated Kaelin's bedroom was. "I looked further along the path and noticed a dark object. . . . It was a right-hand, dark brown leather glove with something slightly wet-looking on it."[12] To Fuhrman, the glove looked like a match for the glove found at the Bundy crime scene, and the wet substance on it appeared to be blood. Leaving it where it was, Fuhrman got Vannatter and showed him the glove. Vannatter decided they should take a closer look for clues in the area surrounding the mansion. Their search soon turned up spots of blood on the driveway that seemed to lead from the Bronco to the mansion. A look inside the Bronco revealed more spots of blood inside the car on the steering wheel, instrument panel, console, and floor. Even though there was no indication of a struggle in the house, the numerous blood spots made Vannatter realize that there were now two crime scenes: Nicole Simpson's Bundy Drive condo and O.J. Simpson's Rockingham Avenue mansion. The evidence was piling up, and it seemed to point to only one person. "You know, Tom," Vannatter said to his partner, "I think Simpson's our suspect."[13] But their suspect was still nowhere to be found.

Finding Simpson

Lange and Phillips knocked on the door of the bungalow next to Kaelin's. Arnelle Simpson, O.J.'s eldest daughter from his marriage to Marguerite, came to the door. "We're looking for your father," Vannatter told her. "Can you tell us where he is?"[14] Arnelle said no, but she could make a call to find out. She led the detectives to the main house and let them in through the back door. There was no sign of a struggle or anything else amiss in the mansion, but neither Simpson nor the maid were there. Arnelle called Cathy Randa, her father's personal assistant. Randa told Arnelle about her father's trip

A Dream of Murder

O.J. Simpson's lawyers may have been called the Dream Team, but a dream of murder had the team in an uproar.

In the early morning hours of June 14, 1994, Simpson, exhausted from a highly emotional day, went to his second-floor bedroom in the Rockingham Avenue mansion. At Simpson's suggestion, Ronald Shipp, a friend and former LAPD officer, followed him upstairs. After the two chatted for a while, the conversation turned to a polygraph test that the police wanted Simpson to take.

"I don't want to take it," Simpson said, "cause I have had some dreams about killing her." Shipp knew that such a statement could result in a false positive on the polygraph, an erroneous indication that Simpson was guilty. But it also could be an admission that Simpson had done it, acting out the subconscious fantasy that manifested itself in his dreams.

During the trial, Judge Lance Ito allowed the jury to hear Shipp's testimony, over the strenuous objections of the defense. It would be up to the jurors to determine if the murder of Nicole Simpson was a dream tragically come true.

Quoted in Sheila Weller, *Raging Heart: The Intimate Story of the Tragic Marriage of O.J. and Nicole Brown Simpson.* New York: Pocket, 1995, p. 11.

to Chicago and gave her the phone number of the hotel where Simpson was staying. Detective Phillips called the number and waited for it to be picked up. When Simpson answered, Phillips identified himself and then said the words that all policemen dread having to say. "I have some bad news for you. Your ex-wife, Nicole Simpson, has been killed."[15] Simpson's immediate reaction was an anguished cry of disbelief. "Oh my God! Nicole is killed? Oh, my God, is she dead?"[16] Phillips

Collecting Blood Samples

Blood evidence found at a crime scene must be carefully collected and preserved to prevent contamination.

1 Bloodstains are first marked with a numbered sign and are photographed. Location, measurements, and a brief description are noted on an evidence collection sheet.

2 A cloth swatch is moistened with distilled water.

3 Using tweezers, the swatch is dabbed on the stain to lift the blood.

4 The swatch is placed in a small bag.

5 The bag is stored in a paper coin envelope, which is labeled with the criminalist's initials and the evidence number. The tweezers are then cleaned.

6 The procedure is repeated in an area next to, but not part of, the bloodstain. This is a "substrate" sample that collects the properties of the surface the blood was on. This sample is stored in a separate plastic bag in the same coin envelope as the stain.

7 Collected evidence is stored in a refrigerated compartment in the crime scene truck and is transported to the lab for examination.

tried to calm Simpson down and explained that his children had been taken to the police station for their safety and that he needed to return home immediately. Simpson vowed to take the next available flight back to Los Angeles. As Phillips hung up, he thought it odd that Simpson had not asked for the details of his ex-wife's death. Was she killed in a traffic accident? Had she died in some sort of violent crime? Did she have an argument with an acquaintance that went terribly wrong? Simpson may have been so distraught that he simply could not verbalize the questions. Or, perhaps he already knew the answer.

Tom Lange had the unenviable job of notifying Nicole Simpson's parents of the murder of their daughter. At 6:21 A.M. he called the Brown residence. Lou Brown, Nicole's father, answered and received the news with stoic calmness. But Denise Brown, Nicole's older sister, had a very different reaction as she listened in on an extension. "He killed her! He finally killed her!" Denise screamed. When Lange asked whom she meant, she replied "O.J."[17]

CHAPTER 2

The Investigation

At approximately 5:30 A.M. on Monday, June 13, 1994, Dennis Fung received a call from a colleague, Andrea Mazzola, informing him of the double homicide of Nicole Simpson and Ron Goldman. The thirty-four-year-old Fung worked as a criminalist in the Scientific Investigation Division of the Los Angeles Police Department (LAPD). A criminalist is an employee of a police department who, in Fung's words, "employs the principles of natural and physical science to identify, document, preserve and analyze evidence that is related to a crime. He later testifies to his findings in a court of law."[18] Fung was a Criminalist 3, an experienced investigator. During the nearly ten years that he had worked at the LAPD, he had processed some five hundred crime scenes. Despite his extensive experience, however, Fung's methods of collecting evidence would come under fire during the Simpson murder trial. Mazzola was a Criminalist 1 for the LAPD, which meant she was still in training. With only four months' practical experience, she had previously worked on only two other crime scenes. Mazzola would collect evidence at the scene under Fung's supervision.

At 7:10 A.M. the two arrived at the Rockingham residence in the LAPD's crime scene truck. Vannatter briefed the criminalists on the situation and gave them a tour of the Rockingham estate. He made special mention of the Bronco parked near the Rockingham Avenue gate and the trail of blood drops on the driveway leading to the entrance of the house. As the lead detective on the case, Vannatter was responsible for everything that happened at the crime scenes, including the actions of the criminalists. He told Fung and

Mazzola, "I want every blood drop, as well as the glove and anything else that's in 'plain view.' I also want the Bronco impounded and towed immediately."[19]

One of Fung's first actions was to take a presumptive test on the blood spot near the door handle of the Bronco. A presumptive test is a quick test of a substance that indicates what the substance probably is or rules out something that it is not. Further testing is needed to confirm the presumptive test's results. Fung performed the test by placing a drop of chemical on the blood spot and waiting for a color change that would indicate the possible presence of blood. When the color changed, he concluded that the stain was most likely blood, although he could not say whose blood it was or even if it was human blood. Upon hearing the result of the presumptive test, Vannatter left the scene and went to the West Los Angeles police station to write out an official search warrant for the Simpson

At the Simpson trial, criminalist Dennis Fung (left) points to a drawing of O.J. Simpson's house indicating where blood drops were found by him during the police investigation. With Fung is defense attorney Barry Scheck.

house. Fung placed an evidence tag bearing the number 1 near the stain on the Bronco, marking it as the first piece of evidence in the Simpson murder case.

Blood Evidence

Fung and Mazzola next began collecting physical evidence, mainly blood samples, from the exterior of the Bronco and from various places on the Rockingham estate. In order to prevent contamination of the samples, and to lessen the health risk when working with bodily fluids, Fung and Mazzola wore rubber gloves during the collection process. Standard procedure dictates that if gloves get too contaminated, or the investigator moves from one part of the crime scene to another, he or she should discard the old gloves and put on new ones. Working as a team, the criminalists collected the stain on the Bronco's door at about 8:15 A.M. and then began concentrating on the blood drops on the driveway. Fung began by collecting the first two bloodstains near the gate and then Mazzola took over. For selected drops of blood, they methodically numbered the samples, had them photographed, measured them, and finally collected the evidence, placing them in evidence containers.

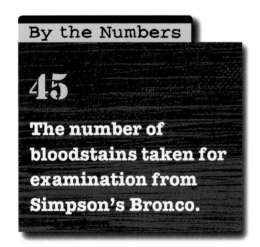

By the Numbers

45

The number of bloodstains taken for examination from Simpson's Bronco.

As they were collecting the samples, Detective Fuhrman walked by and noticed that the criminalists were retrieving only every fourth or fifth drop. Fuhrman was troubled by Fung's collection methods. Even though he had not heard Vannatter's instruction to Fung to recover "every blood drop," he knew that being thorough in every aspect of this investigation was important. Fuhrman approached Fung as he stood on the driveway. "Why don't you recover every drop of blood?" he asked. "It looks like you're missing a lot of drops."[20] Fung answered that a representative sample of the bloodstains was good enough, and that retrieving every drop was

not necessary. Fuhrman worried that perhaps important evidence was being ignored. But since he was not in charge of the case, he had no authority over how the criminalists did their work. Fung and Mazzola continued collecting blood spots from the driveway, from the walkway to Simpson's front door, and from the foyer of the house. In Simpson's upstairs bedroom, Fung collected a pair of dark socks that detectives had found on the carpet at the foot of Simpson's bed. The socks were the only items that were out of place in an otherwise neat bedroom.

This view of the walkway to Nicole Simpson's home on Bundy Drive shows the bloodstained area leading to Nicole's body.

After Fung had finished collecting the blood evidence, Fuhrman led him to the narrow walkway behind the bungalows and showed him the bloody glove he had found earlier. Fung carefully placed the glove in a brown paper bag, numbered the bag, and sealed it. Then Fuhrman pointed out another piece of evidence he had discovered. On the opposite side of the chain-link fence separating the Simpson property from its neighbor, the detective had noticed a small blue plastic bag lying on the ground. While Fung waited, Fuhrman jumped over the fence and retrieved the bag. It was the last piece of evidence the criminalists gathered at the Rockingham location that morning, although they would return later that day. At 10:00 A.M. Fung and Mazzola left Rockingham and drove to the Bundy crime scene.

Another piece of evidence reportedly discovered by Fuhrman was found at the Bundy location. While making his first examination of the crime scene with his partner, Detective Brad Roberts, the two men walked around to the alley behind the condominium. They trained their flashlights on a gate at the rear of the property and noticed several bloody smears, including one bloody fingerprint on the gate's brass latch knob. Fuhrman saw that it was what he considered a high-quality print, one that would be extremely useful to fingerprint technicians. Other items of possible evidentiary value were there behind the condominium, including more blood drops and two coins, a dime and a penny, on the ground next to Nicole Simpson's Jeep Cherokee. But the fingerprint, in Fuhrman's mind, was a crucial clue that could lead to the identity of the killer.

Back inside the condominium, Fuhrman wrote down the discovery of the fingerprint as item number fifteen in his crime scene notes: "15) Rear gate, inside dead bolt (turn knob type) possible blood smudge and visible fingerprint."[21] For all the importance that Fuhrman attached to the bloody fingerprint, his later actions at the crime scene have called this piece of evidence into question. When he turned over his notes to Vannatter and Lange, he did not specifically mention the fingerprint. Neither did he have the crime scene photographer take a picture of it. In fact, the blood on the rear gate of the Bundy residence would not be collected until several weeks later.

The Coroner's Investigators Arrive

Early on the morning of June 13, Detective Phillips placed a call to the Los Angeles County coroner's office to alert it of the double homicide on Bundy Drive. This was a preliminary call, putting the coroner's office on notice that it would soon be needed at the crime scene. Although criminalists like Dennis Fung collect most of the evidence at a crime scene, they cannot touch or remove any evidence from a corpse. Only a coroner or a criminalist from the coroner's office can move a body or recover evidence on or under the body.

While the investigation continued, Lange became concerned about the increasing number of news crews that had been arriving at Bundy. Although kept at a distance by the yellow police tape, the photographers and videographers could use telephoto lenses to get close shots of the crime scene, especially of Nicole Simpson's bloodied body, which was visible to anyone standing on the sidewalk. Publication of such sensational photographs would not only be painful for the victims' families, they might become prejudicial during the trial. Lange asked a uniformed officer to find something in the house that could be used to obscure the view of the bodies. The officer soon returned with a clean, folded blanket that he had found in a bathroom. Carefully, Lange draped the blanket over Simpson's body.

The second call to the coroner was placed just after 8:00 A.M., and at around 9:10 coroner's investigator Claudine Ratcliffe and her assistant, John Jacobo, arrived. After briefly touring the scene, Ratcliffe and Jacobo began inspecting the two bodies, providing the detectives with the first close-up looks at the victims. Preliminary examination revealed that the victims had been stabbed to death, officially known as death by "sharp force injury." Nicole Simpson had been savagely attacked. Her injuries included several stab wounds to her head, a bruise on her scalp, and a fatal knife wound to her neck that was so deep that it cut all the way to her spine. Her hands had several cuts on them, defense wounds indicating that she had held her hands up in a futile effort to ward off the knife blows. The bottoms of Simpson's feet attracted Lange's attention. Although she was not wearing shoes, the soles of her feet were clean, with no signs that she had stepped in blood.

Locard's Principle

In the early twentieth century, the world's first crime lab was established in Lyon, France. Its director was Edmond Locard, a physician and professor of law. Locard, often called "the Sherlock Holmes of France," created the basis for future advances in forensic science, especially in the area of trace evidence. Among other innovations, he developed twelve matching points to be used in comparing fingerprints.

Locard realized that a criminal could not flee a crime scene without leaving minute evidence of his or her presence there. His most famous legacy to forensic science is known as Locard's exchange principle:

Wherever [a criminal] steps, whatever he touches, whatever he leaves, even unconsciously, will serve as a silent witness against him. Not only his fingerprints or his footprints, but his hair, the fibers from his clothes, the glass he breaks, the tool mark he leaves, the paint he scratches, the blood or semen he deposits or collects. All of these and more, bear mute witness against him. . . . Physical evidence cannot be wrong, it cannot perjure itself, it cannot be wholly absent. Only human failure to find it, study and understand it, can diminish its value.

Quoted in Answers.com, "Locard's Exchange Principle." www.answers.com/topic/locard-s-exchange-principle.

Edmond Locard, shown here, was a French physician and criminal jurist who created the forensic exchange principle named for him.

This indicated to Lange that Simpson had somehow been incapacitated before the fatal neck wound was struck.

Now that he was able to see the body close up, Lange noticed a number of small blood drops spattered across Simpson's back. Since there were no wounds on her back, Lange wondered where the blood droplets had come from; perhaps the killer had cut himself during the attacks. This potentially important evidence needed to be collected for further examination, but there was a problem. Ratcliffe and Jacobo were investigators, not criminalists, and only a coroner's criminalist could retrieve the evidence. Lange had no choice but to allow Simpson's body to be removed and hope that the blood spatters would be properly collected later. He made sure, however, that photographs were taken to document the existence of the blood drops.

The investigators then turned to the male victim, who was still unidentified. Examination determined that he was also stabbed to death, with numerous wounds on his body and neck, as well as defense wounds on both hands. There were signs that the victim may have struggled with his assailant: The backs of his hands were bruised (evidence that he may have hit his attacker), and cuts on his boots indicated the possibility that he tried to kick away the knife. A check of a driver's license and credit card recovered from his wallet revealed the man's identity: He was Ron Goldman, Nicole Simpson's friend from Mezzaluna.

Before they were moved, both bodies were photographed so that their positions at the time of death would be documented. Measurements were also taken to record the exact position of the bodies relative to their surroundings and to other objects of evidence at the scene. In a life-or-death struggle, evidence such as dried blood or minute pieces of skin often can be found under a homicide victim's fingernails. Ratcliffe took fingernail samples from Simpson and placed them into a small envelope. She attempted to get samples from Goldman, but his nails were too short. She also took hair samples, which could later be compared to other strands of hair investigators might find among the physical evidence collected. Then the bodies were wrapped in plastic body wrap and placed in the coroner's van to be transported to the coroner's office, the Forensic Science Center. At the center, the bodies would be photographed again and more evidence retrieved, after which autopsies would be performed.

Evidence at Bundy

Fung and Mazzola arrived at the Bundy Drive location around 10:15 A.M. and met with Detective Lange, who showed them around the crime scene. Then Lange showed Fung the various items of evidence that he wanted the criminalist and his assistant to collect. Fung placed a small numbered card next to each piece of evidence to be collected. Then the items were photographed, with the numbered card serving as the identification number in each photograph. Among those items were the ones discovered by the first officers on the scene. Fung and Mazzola recovered the knit cap, the bloodstained envelope, and the bloody left-hand glove. They also retrieved a pager and a set of keys that had belonged to Goldman and a ring that was found under his body. While the detectives were working, Goldman's pager started beeping. It was later learned that it was one of Goldman's friends calling to find out why he never showed up for a drink as was planned for the previous night. Blood samples were taken from the bloodstains on the walkway and the steps leading up to the condominium's entrance. Among the smears of blood that covered the walkway were several bloody shoe prints that showed a distinctive pattern. Fung estimated they were made by a man's size twelve shoe. The pattern did not match the tread on the bottom of Goldman's boots, so the prints could only have been made by one person: the killer.

Simpson Returns

While the Bundy Drive crime scene was being processed, O.J. Simpson, who had taken the next available flight from Chicago, arrived at around noon at his Rockingham estate. He was accompanied by his personal assistant, Cathy Randa; lawyers Howard Weitzman and Skip Taft; and Robert Kardashian, another attorney and Simpson's close friend. By this time, the media had learned of the murders, and photographers and television camera crews were gathered around outside the front gate. Randa and the lawyers were detained at the gate while Simpson walked up the driveway toward his house. Before he reached the front door,

Simpson, with his attorney Howard Weitzman, leaves police headquarters in downtown Los Angeles after being interviewed by detectives.

however, a uniformed officer took Simpson aside and placed handcuffs on him. Vannatter greeted Simpson at the door and, aware that Simpson had not yet been charged with a crime, removed the handcuffs. As he did so, he noticed that the middle finger of Simpson's left hand was bandaged. The detective made a mental note of this potentially important finding.

After talking with Vannatter for a few minutes, Simpson agreed to go with the detectives to the Parker Center, headquarters of the LAPD, so that Vannatter and Lange could question him about his actions over the past twenty-four hours. Simpson, accompanied by his lawyers, went with the detectives willingly. The interview began just after 1:30 P.M. Simpson was alone with the detectives; somewhat surprisingly, the attorneys did not remain with their client, a potential murder suspect, during the questioning. Simpson talked about the dance recital, the limo ride to the airport, his late-night flight to Chicago, and the last time he drove his Bronco. When Vannatter asked about the cut on his finger, Simpson said it had happened while he was in Chicago. "I broke a glass. . . . One of you guys had just called me, and I was in the bathroom, and I just kind of went bonkers for a little bit."[22] Later, however, he contradicted himself, saying he had cut it in Los Angeles the previous night. By the end of the thirty-two-minute interview, Simpson was not giving Lange and Vannatter much useful information, so they ended the session and took Simpson upstairs to be photographed and finger-printed. Lange made sure that Simpson's injured finger was photographically documented. Simpson was taken to the dispensary, where a nurse drew a blood sample with a syringe, then transferred it to a glass vial. The vial contained the chemical EDTA, a preservative that would keep the blood sample fresh until it could be refrigerated. Vannatter took the vial and placed it in an LAPD evidence envelope. He then told Simpson that, for now, there was nothing more the police needed from him, and that he could go home. While the crime scenes at Rockingham Avenue and Bundy Drive were still being investigated, O.J. Simpson, the prime suspect in the murders of Nicole Simpson and Ron Goldman, was still a free man.

According to Vannatter, he now faced a dilemma concerning Simpson's blood sample. He was eager to get it to forensic investigators as soon as possible. But because of the hectic pace of the investigation so far, an official Division of Records (DR) number, required to catalog the evidence, had not been issued. Weighing the choice between getting the sample into the proper hands and doing necessary but time-consuming paperwork, Vannatter made his decision. At 4:20 P.M. he grabbed the envelope containing the vial, got in his car, and headed for the Rockingham crime scene.

A Suspicious Stain

Vannatter arrived back at Rockingham at 5:17 P.M., pushing his way through the growing crowd of media representatives. The detective located criminalist Fung, who was about to wrap up his own work at the crime scene. Vannatter handed the envelope containing the vial of O.J. Simpson's blood to Fung. "Here's a blood sample from Simpson," he explained. "It's part of the evidence package."[23] The blood had been in Vannatter's possession for about two hours. Fung placed the sample in the back of the crime scene van.

While the LAPD was searching for clues in Brentwood, a Chicago police detective was examining O.J. Simpson's hotel room for evidence. At the LAPD's request, Chicago detective Kenneth Berris searched Room 915 at the O'Hare Plaza hotel, where Simpson had spent several hours the night of the murders. In the suite Berris found a broken drinking glass in the bathroom as well as a suspicious red stain on the bedclothes. There was, however, no evidence of blood in the sink. If Simpson really cut himself on the glass as he said, he did not start bleeding until he went into the bedroom. Another peculiarity was that the room contained no laundry bags, perhaps indicating either an oversight by the hotel management or that Simpson

Contaminated by EDTA?

EDTA (ethylenediaminetetraacetic acid) is a versatile chemical compound. Among its many uses, EDTA is a food preservative, a cosmetics stabilizer, and an irrigant in certain dental procedures. It is also an anticoagulant used to preserve blood samples.

When a blood sample was taken from O.J. Simpson at LAPD headquarters, it was placed in a tube that contained EDTA. Detective Philip Vannatter then carried the tube around for several hours before giving it to criminalist Dennis Fung. Defense attorneys argued that Vannatter used that time to frame Simpson by sprinkling the EDTA-laced blood around the crime scenes. Blood spilled from a cut finger, for example, would not contain EDTA; some of the blood spots collected by police tested positive for the chemical. To the defense, this was evidence that the blood drops had been planted from Simpson's sample.

But EDTA is commonly found on environmental surfaces. Blood drops left by Simpson, the prosecution argued, could have picked up the EDTA when they fell. The FBI later said that the blood drops could also have picked up EDTA from water used to clean laboratory equipment.

had carried away something, perhaps evidence, in the bags. Unfortunately, no forensic tests were made on the red stain on the bed or in the sink to determine if it was actually blood.

Red stains were also causing a brief commotion back at Rockingham. Some clothes that had been left in Simpson's washing machine appeared to have bloodstains on them, indicating that Simpson may have tried to wash blood out of his clothes. The excitement quieted down when an examination by Fung revealed that the stains were not blood but simply rust stains from the washer.

It had been a long and grueling day for the detectives, criminalists, photographers, and other crime scene technicians. It was after 7:00 P.M. when Vannatter and Lange signed out, leaving the crime scene secured by yellow tape and uniformed officers. Tired as they were, the detectives felt they had collected enough evidence to make a strong case against Simpson. From his home, Vannatter called Deputy District Attorney Marcia Clark, who would be the lead prosecutor in the trial. Clark had visited the crime scene earlier with Vannatter. "Hey," he said, "I think we've got this thing nailed down pretty good." Clark replied, "It looks like a great case."[24]

CHAPTER 3

Examining the Evidence

After all the evidence was collected from the Bundy and Rockingham residences, prosecutors had to determine how to proceed. As prosecutor Marcia Clark explains, "A case like this—with no eyewitnesses save, possibly, a white Akita—clearly would hinge on physical evidence, especially blood evidence."[25] If it could be proved that O.J. Simpson's blood was at the Bundy Drive crime scene, or that blood from Nicole Simpson or Ron Goldman was found in O.J.'s Bronco or on the glove found at Rockingham, the district attorney's office would have a good chance of winning a conviction in court. Dennis Fung was in his lab in the Piper Technical Center, the Los Angeles Police Department (LAPD) crime lab facility, early on the morning of Tuesday, June 14. On the lab bench in front of him sat some of the pieces of evidence that he and Andrea Mazzola had collected from the crime scenes: the bloody gloves, blood samples taken from the Bundy walkway and the Rockingham driveway, and the vial of O.J.'s blood that Vannatter had given him the day before.

Fung would not be doing the preliminary testing of the evidence. That task fell to Collin Yamauchi, an LAPD criminalist in the serology unit of the Special Investigations Division (SID). According to Yamauchi, "Serology is the unit that specializes in body fluids, most commonly blood and those found in sexual assaults."[26] A five-year veteran of the SID, Yamauchi would analyze the blood samples to determine their sources. Fung showed Yamauchi the various pieces of evidence that he wanted him to test and then left to begin tests on the bloodstains found on the white

Bronco that had been parked at Rockingham the night of the murders.

The Coroner's Examination

Vannatter and Lange met Irwin Golden, the Los Angeles County deputy medical examiner, at the coroner's office near the University of Southern California Medical Center in downtown Los Angeles. Golden led the detectives, dressed in protective gowns, masks, and gloves, into the autopsy room. Before an autopsy of a murder victim is performed, photographs of the body are taken to document the nature, size, and placement of wounds. Any forensic evidence found on the body is collected and booked for further analysis. Then the body is opened and the internal organs are examined and weighed. Slices of various organs may be taken for later microscopic inspection. The coroner usually dictates his or her findings into a recorder as he or she works; this dictation is then used to prepare the written autopsy report. All this information helps authorities determine the cause, manner, and, in some cases, the estimated time of death.

The attack on Nicole Simpson was so savage that the cause of death was apparent. The massive neck wound had severed the two carotid arteries and one of two jugular veins that bring blood to the head and brain. The resulting massive bleeding would have caused her death within a matter of minutes. One piece of evidence did not appear on Simpson's autopsy report: The blood splatters on her back that Lange had noticed had been washed away when the body was being prepared for examination. The autopsy of Ron Goldman revealed many nonfatal stab wounds on his head and neck, which could have been inflicted for the purpose of taunting the victim and causing extreme pain. Fatal stab wounds were found in Goldman's chest and abdomen, the latter severing the abdominal aorta, the major artery in the abdomen. Golden estimated that the time of death was somewhere between 9:00 P.M. and midnight.

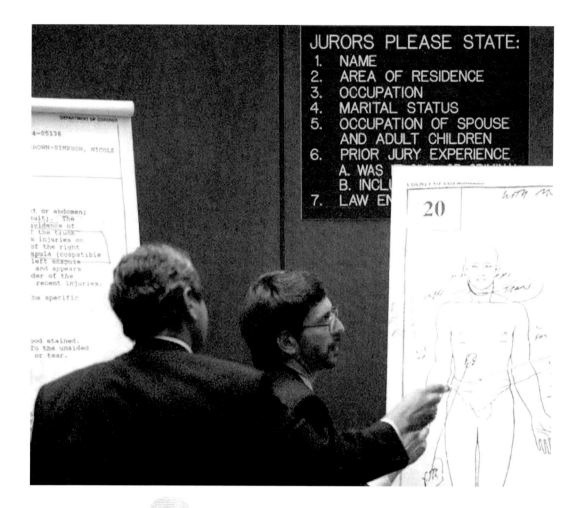

JURORS PLEASE STATE:
1. NAME
2. AREA OF RESIDENCE
3. OCCUPATION
4. MARITAL STATUS
5. OCCUPATION OF SPOUSE AND ADULT CHILDREN
6. PRIOR JURY EXPERIENCE
   A. WAS
   B. INCL
7. LAW EN

Los Angeles County coroner Lakshmanan Sathyavagiswaran points to wounds on an autopsy diagram of Nicole Brown Simpson during the murder trial.

Testing DNA

Collin Yamauchi began his testing of the blood samples the morning of Tuesday, June 14, in the serology unit of the LAPD lab. Dennis Fung had shown Yamauchi which samples should be tested: blood drops from the Bundy walkway and from the alley behind the Bundy condominium, reference samples of Nicole Simpson's and Ron Goldman's blood taken from the crime scene, the socks found in O.J. Simpson's bedroom, the vial of O.J.'s blood, and the glove found at the Rockingham location. Yamauchi's first order of business was to prepare a sample of O.J.'s blood from the vial that would be used as a reference for the rest of his tests. Yamauchi, wearing latex gloves, picked up the vial, noting that there was enough blood to be used in the test, but not measuring the exact amount of blood in the tube. When he removed the cap, a small amount of the blood got onto Yamauchi's gloves and on some tissues he had placed over the vial. Discarding the tissues and replacing the contaminated gloves, Yamauchi continued the test. He used a pipette to place several drops of blood on a Fitzco card, which is used to store exemplars, or reference blood samples. Setting the Fitzco card aside to allow the blood to dry, Yamauchi placed the cap back on the vial and started the testing process for the DNA in the collected blood samples.

Deoxyribonucleic acid (DNA) is the genetic blueprint that each person carries in almost every cell of his or her body. Genes in the DNA determine what a person looks like, what his or her personality is, and how each of the trillions of cells in the body should function. Everyone's DNA is unique and thus, like fingerprints, it can be used to identify a person. Several tests have been developed that can be used to compare DNA from an unidentified source to reference DNA samples. Yamauchi conducted a test known as polymerase chain reaction (PCR) on the blood drops found on the walkway at Bundy Drive. The PCR test is a simple and quick method of obtaining comparisons between known and unknown blood samples. Although the PCR test can achieve results from the very smallest quantities of blood, its accuracy is limited and additional tests are usually performed to confirm the PCR results. At the time of the Simpson and Goldman murders, PCR testing was new, and not all states allowed the results to be admitted as evidence. But there was a good reason to use the PCR test, as

By the Numbers

6,000

The approximate number of autopsies performed annually by the Los Angeles County coroner's office.

Marcia Clark explains: "With the suspect at large, it was crucial to get this screening test done quickly. If the preliminary markers linked Simpson to the crime scene, the police would have plenty of grounds to arrest."[27]

Another more established type of test is known as restriction fragment length polymorphism (RFLP). This test requires a greater amount of DNA than the PCR test does, and takes longer to perform, but it is much more accurate. RFLP testing can narrow a person's identity down to odds of one in a million or even higher. The LAPD lab was not equipped to perform RFLP tests, so blood samples were sent to Cellmark Diagnostics, a private laboratory in Maryland that was able to handle the most sophisticated DNA testing.

Collin Yamauchi spent the better part of two days performing his tests, which were known as PCR DQ-alpha. Early results from the tests he performed on Tuesday were encouraging. The blood drops taken from the Bundy walkway matched O.J. Simpson's blood type; only 7 percent of the population had this type of blood. When prosecutor Marcia Clark heard the results, she was elated. "There was the evidence the cops needed to charge. . . . I figured squad cars would be rolling toward Brentwood any minute now."[28] Even the news media somehow learned of the test results and soon were broadcasting them to the nation. These test results were preliminary, and they would have to be confirmed by the RFLP tests being done at Cellmark, which would take several weeks.

While Yamauchi was testing the blood evidence in the police lab, Simpson was changing lawyers. Howard Weitzman, who had accompanied Simpson when he returned from Chicago on June 13, announced that he was withdrawing from representing Simpson because of their friendship and due to his obligations to other clients. He was replaced by Robert Shapiro, a fifty-one-year-old criminal defense attorney. When he took over the case, Shapiro based his strategy on cooperation and building trust with the police. He offered the services of two forensic experts he had retained—criminalist Henry

Henry Lee, Forensic Authority

If the field of forensics could be said to have a superstar, that man would surely be Henry Lee. He was born in China but later immigrated to the United States, where he earned a bachelor's degree in forensic science in 1972 and a doctorate in biochemistry in 1975. That same year Lee volunteered to help the Connecticut State Police develop a forensic laboratory and assist in criminal investigations.

In addition to the O.J. Simpson case, Lee has investigated numerous other high-profile cases, including the 1996 murder of six-year-old JonBenét Ramsey, the Laci Peterson homicide, and the suicide of White House counsel Vincent Foster. Lee has investigated more than four thousand homicides and has testified as a witness in more than one thousand civil and criminal cases. He is an expert in forensic serology, fingerprint matching, ballistics, and crime scene reconstruction.

After thirty-five years of experience, Lee is now chief emeritus of the Connecticut State Police Laboratory. He has written numerous books and articles on forensic science.

Noted forensics expert Henry Lee simulates blood patterns by using ink drops as he addresses the jury during the trial.

Lee and pathologist Michael Baden—to assist the police in their investigation. The LAPD politely declined the offer. Shapiro also had Simpson undergo a polygraph, or lie detector, test in which Simpson scored a minus twenty-two, meaning he failed nearly all the questions put to him.

Two Funerals

On Thursday, June 16, the funerals of Nicole Simpson and Ron Goldman were held under clear Southern California skies. After a service at St. Martin of Tours Catholic Church in Brentwood, Simpson was laid to rest at Ascension Cemetery in Lake Forest, Orange County, California. O.J. Simpson and his children were at the graveside service, as were many of O.J.'s friends, including Al "A.C." Cowlings, who had been his teammate throughout his high school, college, and professional football careers. Several family photographs adorned the casket, some that had been taken by Nicole herself. When the service ended, O.J., dressed in a dark suit and wearing sunglasses, hugged the members of the Brown family. After a reception at the Browns' home, Simpson left, evidently to return to his Rockingham estate.

The service for Ron Goldman took place at the Valley Oaks Memorial Park in Westlake Village. In the chapel, loving memories of Goldman were tearfully recounted by family members and friends. Rabbi Gary Johnson offered prayers. Later, at the grave site, hundreds of Goldman's friends and acquaintances watched as Goldman's father, stepmother, and sister, Kim, each dropped a handful of earth in turn on the casket as it was lowered into the ground. The entire proceeding was covered by more than twenty news media camera crews.

Warrant for Arrest

That same day detectives Lange and Vannatter were at LAPD headquarters, trying to determine if they had enough evidence to charge Simpson with two counts of murder. That afternoon they received word that Yamauchi had completed his examination of the stains on the Rockingham glove and had found a mixture of blood belonging to O.J. Simpson, Nicole Simpson, and Ron Goldman. This evidence linked the glove found behind Kato Kaelin's room to O.J. and both murder victims. It was the confirmation that the detectives needed, and they began the paperwork that would culminate in an arrest warrant for O.J. Simpson.

Shapiro had already met with the police and, maintaining his cooperative mood, assured them that if and when a warrant

At a press conference, Detectives Tom Lange (left) and Philip Vannatter announce they have filed homicide charges against O.J. Simpson.

was issued, he would have Simpson surrender to the authorities. This would avoid the necessity of having to go out and arrest Simpson, a situation that would just provide more sensational fodder for the already frenzied media that were now covering the case nonstop. So the plan was set. At 11:00 A.M. on Friday, June 17, Simpson would surrender to the LAPD at the Parker Center. He would then be taken to the Criminal Courts Building a few blocks away for his arraignment. It was a simple plan, but even simple plans can fall apart.

On Friday morning Vannatter and Lange filed the case with the Los Angeles County district attorney's office. The charge was homicide with special circumstances, the term referring to the fact that it was a double homicide. These special circumstances allowed the police to hold Simpson without bail and made him eligible for the death penalty, if the prosecution decided to seek it. At 8:30 Lange telephoned Shapiro at his home to officially inform him of the warrant. "Mr. Shapiro," Lange said, "we are getting a warrant for Mr. Simpson's arrest . . . and we want your full cooperation. Like you, we want to avoid a media circus."[29] Shapiro was concerned because Simpson was extremely depressed, but he said that he would have his client at the Parker Center on time.

Simpson was not at his Rockingham estate; instead, he was at the home of a close friend, Robert Kardashian, in Encino, some 20 miles (32.2km) from the LAPD headquarters. More than a dozen people filled the house, including O. J.'s friend A.C. Cowlings, a physician and a psychiatrist, forensic experts Dr. Henry Lee and Dr. Michael Baden, Kardashian and his girlfriend, and O. J.'s girlfriend Paula Barbieri. Shapiro drove there to give Simpson the bad news in person. "O.J. the police have called," Shapiro said quietly. "You have to turn yourself in today. They're going to charge you with double murder and you have to surrender yourself by eleven o'clock this morning."[30] Simpson's reaction was one of disbelief. "I can't understand why they aren't looking for other people. Two people had to do something like this. I don't understand why this is being blamed on me."[31]

After dressing, Simpson went to the second-floor study and began making phone calls and writing on legal pads. He finalized some business matters, arranged for the Browns to take custody of Justin and Sydney, wrote personal letters to his mother and children, and modified his will. Lee and Baden took blood, hair, and skin samples from Simpson and took photographs of him (including close-ups of the cut on his finger), which the defense would use in compiling its case for Simpson's innocence. After observing Simpson's demeanor for a few minutes, the psychiatrist told Shapiro that the police should put him on a suicide watch once they had him in jail.

At the Parker Center, the detectives were watching the clock. At 11:00 A.M. there was no sign of Simpson or his lawyer. It was soon 11:30, then noon, and still no Simpson. By 12:50 the police had had enough. They dispatched two black-and-white patrol cars to the Kardashian residence. Arriving at the house, the officers informed Kardashian that they were there to pick up Simpson. But when Kardashian went upstairs to inform his friend, he could not find Simpson anywhere. The officers searched the house, but Simpson was nowhere to be found.

At the Parker Center, the phone rang. A detective answered and, after listening for a minute, hung up and turned to Vannatter and Lange. "Simpson's gone. . . . He's taken off with A.C. Cowlings."[32] An all-points bulletin was issued for Cowlings, who was driving a white Ford Bronco almost identical to Simpson's. Police also alerted officers in jurisdictions adjacent to Los Angeles County through which the escaping fugitives might travel.

Chasing Simpson

At 2:00 P.M. LAPD commander David Gascon held a news conference at the Parker Center. "Mr. Simpson," he began, "in agreement with his attorney, was scheduled to surrender this morning to the Los Angeles Police Department. . . . Mr. Simpson has not appeared. The Los Angeles Police

As A.C. Cowlings drives O.J. Simpson through the freeways of Los Angeles during the slow-speed police chase, crowds of supporters cheer Simpson on.

Department right now is actively searching for Mr. Simpson. . . . [He] is out there and we will find him."[33]

At 6:45 P.M. an Orange County deputy sheriff driving on Interstate 5 south of Los Angeles spotted a white Bronco pulling onto the freeway. The deputy followed the Bronco and called in the license plate number. Dispatch soon confirmed that the Bronco was indeed Cowlings's. Inside the Bronco, Cowlings dialed 911 on his cell phone. "This is A.C.," he said. "I've got O.J. in the car. Right now . . . we're all okay, but you got to tell the police to just back off. He's still alive. He's got a gun to his head."[34] Cowlings said that he was taking Simpson back to his Rockingham estate. What happened next was a bizarre slow-speed highway chase, viewed live on television by some 95 million Americans. By 7:00 police and television helicopters buzzed overhead as Cowlings's Bronco drove north on the freeway, followed by patrol cars from the LAPD, Orange County Sheriff's Department, and the California Highway Patrol. Cowlings did not try to outrun the police; he kept his speed between 30 and 50 miles per hour (48.3 and 80.5 kph). Similarly, the police did not try to intercept the Bronco, fearing Simpson might take his life. As the Bronco led the chase through Los Angeles County on Interstate 405, people lined overpasses along the route, holding signs and shouting "Go, O.J.!" and "Save the Juice!"[35]

Detective Lange was watching the chase on the office television at LAPD headquarters. Realizing that he had Simpson's cell phone number, he grabbed a phone and dialed. Soon Simpson's voice came on the line, the sounds of sirens wailing in the background: "I swear to you I'll give you me. . . . I just need to get to my house where I lived with Nicole." Lange replied, "Okay. We're gonna do that. Just throw the gun out the window." Simpson was distraught, moaning and sobbing. "I can't do that."[36] Lange kept him on the line, trying desperately to calm him down and get him to toss the gun out the window. But Simpson would not listen, and the slow chase continued.

End of the Road

The Bronco left the interstate and made its way through the streets of Los Angeles, heading toward Brentwood and Simpson's home. At around 7:50 P.M. Cowlings finally pulled the Bronco into the Ashford Street gate of Simpson's estate. Waiting there was a SWAT team dressed in battle gear and armed with automatic weapons, stun grenades, and night-vision scopes. When the Bronco rolled to a stop, however, no one emerged. The next hour was a standoff between the police and the two occupants of the Bronco. Media helicopters circled overhead, and crowds beyond the property's gates shouted encouragement to Simpson. A police negotiator, talking to Simpson on his cell phone, pleaded with the athlete to surrender for the sake of his children and his mother.

Simpson's Suicide Note

Before Simpson began his slow-speed Bronco chase, he left his friend Robert Kardashian a sealed letter. When Kardashian read it before a crowd of reporters, Simpson's words sounded like those of a man planning to take his own life. Here are excerpts from that letter:

I've had a good life. I'm proud of how I lived. My mama taught me to do unto others. I treated people the way I wanted to be treated. I've always tried to be up and helpful. So why is this happening? I'm sorry for the Goldman family. I know how much it hurts. . . .

Nicole and I had a good life together. All this press talk about a rocky relationship was no more than what every long-term relationship experiences. All her friends will confirm that I have been totally loving and understanding of what she's been going through. At times, I have felt like a battered husband or boyfriend, but I loved her; make that clear to everyone. And I would take whatever it took to make it work.

Don't feel sorry for me. I've had a great life, great friends. Please think of the real O.J. and not this lost person.

Thanks for making my life special. I hope I helped yours.

Peace and love, O.J.

Quoted in CNN, "O.J.'s Suicide Note." www.cnn.com/US/OJ/suspect/note.

Finally, at 8:53 P.M., the Bronco's door opened and Simpson stepped out. He was holding some family photographs that he had apparently been looking at during the slow-speed chase. He walked in the front door of his house and told police, "I'm sorry, guys. I'm sorry I put you through this."[37] Police searched the Bronco and found in Simpson's travel bag several items that could be used for a disguised escape: $8,750 in cash, Simpson's passport, a phony mustache and beard, and bottles of makeup adhesive and remover. They also recovered Simpson's gun, a Smith and Wesson .357 magnum. After allowing Simpson to talk to his mother on the phone, police handcuffed him and walked him to a waiting car for the trip downtown to the Parker Center to begin the next phase of his life as O.J. Simpson, defendant.

CHAPTER 4

The Trial of the Century

Before a trial date could be set for Simpson, the court had to review the evidence and decide whether there was probable cause to try him for the murders. This was done by holding a preliminary hearing in open court. During a preliminary hearing, the prosecution presents its case; the defense can cross-examine prosecution witnesses and learn what evidence the prosecution has, so it can begin to prepare its case.

The Preliminary Hearing

Judge Kathleen Kennedy-Powell convened the preliminary hearing on June 30. Preliminary hearings are held in public, and in the Simpson case the hearing received national television coverage. Preliminary hearings do not have juries; the decision to indict is made by the presiding judge. For six days the prosecution laid out its case for Judge Kennedy-Powell. The defense presented its own arguments and cross-examined prosecution witnesses in an attempt to discredit the prosecution's evidence. On July 8 Judge Kennedy-Powell made her decision. "Keeping in mind that the proof in this matter is not proof beyond a reasonable doubt," the judge said, "the court feels that there is ample evidence to establish strong suspicion of the guilt of the accused."[38] The prosecution had made its initial case, and now Simpson would stand trial for double homicide.

Two weeks later, on July 22, Simpson was once again in court for a second arraignment. Unlike the Simpson in the aftermath of the slow-speed Bronco chase, he now appeared self-assured and outgoing, wearing an expensive suit. Judge Cecil Mills asked him, "How do you plead?" Simpson's reply echoed throughout the courtroom: "Absolutely, one hundred percent not guilty."[39] As he was escorted by deputies back to his cell, he acknowledged his supporters with a smile and a thumbs-up gesture. Accused of the brutal killing of his wife and her friend, Simpson seemed confident that the outcome of the impending trial would go his way.

The Players

The *State of California v. Orenthal James Simpson* began on January 24, 1995, in a surprisingly small wood-paneled courtroom on the ninth floor of the Los Angeles Criminal Courts Building. Presiding over the trial was Judge Lance A. Ito, a forty-four-year-old Japanese American whose parents had been confined to a Wyoming internment camp during World War II. Ito had a reputation for thoughtfulness and strict judicial rulings as well as a sometimes odd sense of humor. During the trial, he would also show a tendency to become captivated by all the media attention. A former prosecutor, Ito was appointed to the bench in 1987 and had presided over several important cases, including a high-profile savings and loan scandal. He was named trial judge of the year in 1992.

The prosecution was headed up by Marcia Clark and Christopher Darden, a fifteen-year veteran in the Los Angeles County district attorney's office. The prosecution team also included prosecutor William Hodgman (who would later drop out of the case for health reasons) and attorneys Rockne Harmon, George Clarke, Scott Gordon, and Brian Kelberg. Defending Simpson was the so-called Dream Team of lawyers headed by Robert Shapiro and Johnnie Cochran, who, like Shapiro, counted many celebrities among his clients. Simpson's friend Robert Kardashian was also on the team as well as noted attorneys F. Lee Bailey and Alan Dershowitz, lawyer and professor Gerald Uelmen, and two lawyers who were experts in DNA evidence, Barry Scheck and Peter Neufeld. The Dream Team had years of defense experience and vast resources of legal expertise to call on. But all that mattered little if they could not convince the jury of Simpson's innocence.

The prosecution team for the Simpson trial was led by Christopher Darden, left, Marcia Clark, and William Hodgman. Hodgman would have to drop out of the case later.

On December 8 a panel of twelve jurors and twelve alternates was chosen. Due to the extensive media coverage of the Simpson case, the jury would be sequestered in a nearby hotel for the duration of the trial. For a variety of reasons, in the coming months ten of the original jurors would be replaced by alternates. The final jury that would decide Simpson's fate included eight African American women, one African American man, two Hispanic men, and two white women. The racial makeup of the jury concerned prosecutor Christopher Darden. "It wasn't that I didn't want black jurors," Darden later wrote. "But Cochran had made it clear that this was going to be a case based on the fact that O.J. Simpson was black. That's what a predominantly black jury meant; more encouragement for Cochran to . . . turn a murder case into a bogus retribution for past injustices."[40] Despite Darden's misgivings, the jury was set, and the trial could begin.

Opening Acts

In a trial, the prosecution is first to present the facts of its case for the jury in its opening statement. All eyes in the hushed courtroom were on Christopher Darden as he stood up and greeted the members of the jury. Then he began to explain why O.J. Simpson was the killer, pacing nervously in front of the jury box. "You think, 'Why would he do it? Not the O.J. Simpson we've all known for years'. . . . But like many men, he has a private face as well . . . the face of a batterer, a wife-beater, abuser, controller. . . . He killed Nicole for a single reason—one as old as man himself—jealousy. He could not stand losing her so he murdered her."[41] Darden spoke for an hour, taking the story of O.J. and Nicole up to Sydney's dance recital on June 12. Then Marcia Clark took her turn. In her usual businesslike manner, Clark walked the jury through the events of that evening, illustrating her words with crime scene photos projected on a large screen. Then she got to the heart of the prosecution's argument: the forensic evidence. She presented picture after picture of blood spots, each time announcing, "Matches the defendant."[42] She talked about the glove found at Rockingham, which had the blood of O.J., Nicole, and Goldman on it. And she emphasized that O.J. Simpson had no alibi for the time of the murders on that fateful night.

> ### By the Numbers
>
> # 266
>
> **The number of days the Simpson jurors were sequestered.**

The next day Johnnie Cochran used the defense's opening statement to cast doubt on the prosecution's forensic evidence and the methods used to collect and store it.

We are . . . going to talk to you about this evidence, what we call the lack of integrity of much of the prosecution's evidence. . . . [Our experts] will come in here and tell you about this evidence, how sensitive it is and how these police departments are not trained in the collection and use of it. . . . And so the collection of the evidence becomes very, very, very important.[43]

Cochran also suggested that there was a "rush to judgment" on the part of the LAPD, which from the beginning

Marcia Clark for the Prosecution

Marcia Rachel Clark was born on August 31, 1953, in Berkeley, California, the daughter of an Israeli immigrant. After dabbling with the thought of becoming an actress, Clark turned to the study of law. She received her law degree in 1979 and began her career in criminal defense, spending two years as a law clerk and two years as an attorney. In 1981 Clark joined the Los Angeles office of the district attorney, where she prosecuted thousands of cases of all types, from drunk driving to murder. Several of these cases involved the death penalty.

Even before the O.J. Simpson trial, Clark had prosecuted a celebrity case. In 1991 she won a murder conviction for Robert John Bardo, a stalker who had murdered rising young actress Rebecca Schaeffer. In 1993 Clark prosecuted a double homicide case that featured a mountain of forensic evidence. It was an appropriate rehearsal for the O.J. Simpson murder trial.

After the Simpson trial, Clark wrote a book about her experiences in prosecuting the celebrity defendant. For this book, titled *Without a Doubt*, she received a $4 million advance, one of the largest advances in nonfiction publishing history.

considered Simpson as the only suspect, not even looking for other possible killers. He also brought the racial aspect into the case, quoting Martin Luther King Jr. and suggesting that Mark Fuhrman, a detective with a history of prejudice, had played a pivotal role in the investigation.

The Experts Take the Stand

During the first ten weeks of the trial the prosecution presented witnesses who built a strong case for Simpson being the murderer. Denise Brown, Nicole Simpson's sister, recounted stories of O.J. physically abusing Nicole. Kato Kaelin testified about his run to McDonald's with Simpson and the later thumps on the wall of his room. Testimony from detectives Mark Fuhrman, Ron Phillips, Philip Vannatter, and Tom Lange recalled their actions on the night of the murders. After Clark questioned Detective Fuhrman, defense lawyer F. Lee Bailey accused him in cross-examination of planting evidence. "Did you wipe a glove in the Bronco, Detective Fuhrman?"[44] Bailey's theory was that Fuhrman had found two gloves at the Bundy location, had secretly taken one to Rockingham and had wiped blood from the glove on the interior of the Bronco, and then hid the glove behind Kaelin's room to be discovered later. Fuhrman said he had done no such thing, but the idea that he might have planted evidence incriminating Simpson was now before the jury. Bailey continued his verbal assault, asking if the detective had ever used a particularly vile epithet when referring to African Americans. Again, Fuhrman said no, an answer that would come back to haunt the prosecution.

Vannatter was cross-examined by defense counsel Robert Shapiro, who criticized his handling of the crime scene and blood evidence. Shapiro zeroed in on several misstatements that Vannatter had made in writing out the search warrant affidavit for the Rockingham location. Why, Shapiro asked, did Vannatter spend so much time at the Rockingham location when the primary crime scene was at the Bundy residence? He then brought up how Vannatter had carried Simpson's blood sample to Rockingham to give to Fung instead of immediately booking it as evidence at headquarters:

> Shapiro: You just have this blood in your car. Wasn't there a risk of something happening to the blood in transporting it that distance?
>
> Vannatter: No. The risk was me not keeping control of the blood, the chain of custody of the blood to give it to the criminalist. That was the risk.[45]

Shapiro wanted to get across to the jury that Vannatter had been careless with Simpson's blood, causing it to deteriorate and thus become unreliable for DNA testing. There was also the implication that the blood could have been used to plant the blood drops on the Rockingham driveway.

Criminalist Fung took the stand on April 3. After the prosecution's direct examination, he was relentlessly cross-examined by Barry Scheck, one of the defense's DNA experts. For nine days Scheck questioned him about the minute details of his evidence collection, whether he had always worn rubber gloves, and how often he changed his tweezers. Fung admitted that the less experienced Andrea Mazzola had collected most of the blood samples, although always under his supervision. Scheck brought up the blanket that Detective Lange had put over Nicole Simpson's body; Fung acknowledged that it could have transferred hairs from O.J., who had often stayed at the Bundy residence, to the body of Nicole. The prosecution watched in dismay as Scheck pummeled the criminalist with accusations of incompetence and complicity in a plan to frame Simpson. But the final disappointment came as Fung left the witness stand for the last time. As he walked by the defense table, he was greeted with smiles, hugs,

By the Numbers

$9 MILLION

The total cost to Los Angeles County for the trial.

Johnnie Cochran, Captain of the Dream Team

Born in Shreveport, Louisiana, on October 2, 1937, Johnnie L. Cochran Jr. received his undergraduate degree from the University of Los Angeles and his law degree from Loyola Marymount University School of Law. He was inspired by the work of Supreme Court justice Thurgood Marshall to use his skills as a lawyer to change society.

After a time as a deputy city attorney in Los Angeles, Cochran established a private practice in 1965. Although he lost his first important case (the police shooting of a civilian), he realized that it enlightened the community to the problem of the police abuse of minorities. He spent the next several years litigating police brutality cases.

Cochran was voted criminal trial lawyer of the year in 1977, and in 1978 he became the first African American assistant district attorney in Los Angeles County. Five years later he returned to private practice. With his theatrical courtroom manner and flamboyant lifestyle, Cochran attracted many celebrity clients, including Michael Jackson, actor Todd Bridges, and Sean "Diddy" Combs.

Johnnie Cochran died of a brain tumor on March 29, 2005.

Johnnie Cochran, shown here during the Simpson trial, managed to create reasonable doubt in the minds of jurors.

Dealing the prosecution a crucial blow with his testimony, criminalist Dennis Fung, left, is greeted and thanked by Simpson and his defense team.

and handshakes by the attorneys. Even Simpson shook Fung's hand. Fung had performed disastrously for the prosecution, but the defense loved him.

DNA on Trial

The most complicated testimony—and the most mind-numbing for the jury—concerned the DNA tests performed by the various labs to which the prosecution had sent blood samples. By now the trial was in its sixteenth week, and the jury was growing weary of listening to testimony and was fed up with being sequestered. The defense knew that the prosecution's DNA evidence was strong. "We realized going in," comments Gerald Uelmen,

> that there were people who would say, "It's all over, the DNA tests are conclusive." And we knew that we weren't going to be able to keep the DNA evidence out. So our whole approach was, you can't trust DNA test results if you had incompetent people collecting the evidence and preserving the evidence. . . . So our focus had to be on doubts about the integrity of the evidence-collecting process.[46]

For the prosecution, it was time to present its most important evidence. "The star of our DNA case," says Clark, "was Dr. Robin Cotton, a petite woman with short blond hair and wire-rimmed glasses. She was indubitably honest, and her explanations of the very complicated procedures of DNA resting were as simple as one could humanly make them."[47] Cotton was the director of Cellmark Diagnostics, where most of the highly accurate RFLP testing was performed. Cotton testified that she compared the DNA characteristics of the Bundy blood drops to the characteristics in the blood sample taken from Simpson. Prosecutor George Clarke asked her the critical question:

> Clarke: Does that mean that these characteristics that Mr. Simpson has that are also found in the Bundy walk blood stain are only found in approximately 1 out of 170 million Caucasians or African-Americans?
>
> Cotton: Yes, approximately.[48]

The odds were overwhelming that the blood drops on the Bundy walkway were Simpson's. The characteristics of the blood on the socks found in Simpson's bedroom were even more damaging. Cotton said that the blood could have come from only 1 in 6.8 billion people. And that blood matched

Becoming a Criminalist

Job Description:
A criminalist documents a crime scene through photographs and sketches; identifies, collects, and analyzes evidence; and reports findings to investigators for trial preparation.

Education:
Requirements differ depending on the law enforcement agency. Most large police departments require a two- or four-year degree, preferably in the physical sciences or forensics.

Qualifications:
A criminalist must be physically fit to be able to work in the often difficult conditions presented by crime scenes. Above-average proficiency in communication, both written and oral, is necessary, as are deductive reasoning skills and the ability to operate and maintain scientific equipment.

Additional Information:
Some criminalists are police officers, but others are civilians working for the police department. Civilian employees often have lower pay and fewer advancement opportunities.

Salary:
Averages from $20,000 to $50,000 per year.

Nicole Simpson's blood. Cotton also addressed the concern about blood samples being degraded due to improper handling. She stated that even if the blood samples had been degraded (as might have occurred in Vannatter's delay in turning over O.J.'s sample), blood from one person would not appear to be from someone else. The tests would still be valid.

The DNA evidence placed O.J. Simpson at the Bundy residence on the night of the murders and placed Nicole's blood on the socks found in O.J.'s bedroom. The DNA evidence greatly strengthened the prosecution's case. Still, more prosecution witnesses were brought to the stand. When criminalist Collin Yamauchi testified, he created a furor among the prosecution team when he stated that, at the beginning of the investigation, he thought that O.J.'s trip to Chicago provided him with an alibi. The defense accused Yamauchi of sloppy work when handling the forensic evidence. Also brought to the stand was FBI agent William Bodziak, an expert on shoe impressions. Bodziak testified that bloody shoeprints found at the Bundy crime scene were made by a size twelve Bruno Magli shoe, the kind and size of shoes that O.J. had owned.

All the forensic evidence seemed to confirm the prosecution's case against Simpson. But a mistake by prosecutor Christopher Darden thrust all that into doubt.

The Gloves

One of the key pieces of evidence was the bloody glove found behind Kato Kaelin's room at Rockingham. It was a brown Aris Isotoner Leather Light glove, size extra large, and it matched the glove found at the Bundy location. A receipt from Bloomingdale's in Los Angeles showed that Nicole Simpson had bought two pairs of the same type of glove for O.J. in 1990. Darden wanted Simpson to try on the gloves to show the jury that they actually fit his hands. Marcia Clark had warned Darden that the gloves, being old and covered in blood, might have shrunk, but he pressed on. Simpson stood and tried to put on one glove, but he struggled with it, claiming it was too tight. Darden now became nervous that his demonstration was in trouble. "Your Honor," he said to Judge Ito, "apparently Mr. Simpson seems to be having a problem putting the glove on his hand."[49]

Darden handed Simpson the other glove. Simpson again made a great show of not being able to put the glove on. He held his hand up to the jury to demonstrate that the gloves, even though they were extra large size, were too small. But it seemed that Simpson was holding his hands in an awkward position, perhaps making sure that the gloves would not fit. Darden noticed this peculiar action and asked to have him straighten his fingers, but the gloves still did not fit. The prosecution felt Simpson's difficulty with the gloves was just a show. After all, he had been an actor; now perhaps he was acting as if his life depended on it. On the witness stand, a former Aris Isotoner executive said that an extra large size glove

O.J. Simpson attempts to put on a leather glove used in the murders. Johnnie Cochran came up with the catch phrase, "If it doesn't fit, you must acquit."

should have fit Simpson. But the jury had seen otherwise, and the prosecution's case had suffered a major setback.

On July 6 the prosecution rested its case. It was now the defense's turn.

Defending Simpson

The defense's case hinged on several assumptions that it intended to prove in court. First, it argued that, by nature, Simpson could not have done such a terrible thing to the mother of his children, that he was not angry during Sydney's dance recital, but in fact was smiling and chatting with the Brown family. Further, the defense contended that, considering Simpson's arthritis and old football injuries, he physically could not have done it. They brought up the possibility that there may have been someone besides Simpson at the Bundy crime scene, and that other person could be the murderer. And the defense hammered at the incompetence of the investigators and the possibility of a conspiracy in which evidence had been planted at Rockingham and in the Bronco in order to frame Simpson.

The defense brought to the stand its own forensic experts. Michael Baden testified that Nicole Simpson and Ron Goldman had bravely fought off their attacker for some minutes, indicating that their deaths could have occurred later than the police believed. "My opinion," Baden said, "is that [Nicole] struggled with the assailant or assailants prior to succumbing when her neck was cut."[50] Goldman put up a fierce fight as well, possibly kicking his attacker. This extended time, rather than the swift, precise attack the prosecution believed happened, provided an alibi for Simpson. Baden also claimed that the coroner's office had made numerous errors during Nicole's and Goldman's autopsies. These mistakes, he said, led the LAPD to make unwarranted assumptions about how many attackers there were, how many murder weapons were involved, and other details of the two deaths.

Henry Lee also tore into the prosecution's evidence, citing numerous errors in collecting and handling the evidence. Referring to blood samples he had examined in the LAPD crime lab, Lee stated in his Chinese-accented English, "Only opinion I can give under these circumstances—something wrong."[51] He said that the investigators at the crime scene had missed a shoeprint that did not match the Bruno Magli prints, suggesting the presence of a second killer. He testified that he found bloodstains in the Rockingham foyer that the police did not recover and evidence of blood smearing on a bag containing Goldman's shoes. It was this kind of sloppy forensic work, the defense contended, that caused contamina-

> **By the Numbers**
>
> **$36,000**
>
> **The cost to keep Simpson in jail during the trial.**

Blue Jeans

Imprint 1

Imprint 2

Imprint 3

As part of a defense ploy to discredit evidence, Henry Lee explains the possible meanings of shoe imprints found at the murder scene.

tion in the blood evidence and thus made the prosecution's forensic tests unreliable.

Discrediting the forensic evidence was only part of the defense's strategy. It still had one more card up its sleeve: the race card.

A Racist Cop

Laura Hart McKinny was a documentary film producer and writer. In 1985 she happened to meet Mark Fuhrman at an outdoor café, and the two struck up a conversation. When McKinny told Fuhrman that she was working on a screenplay about women in law enforcement, he mentioned that he was with the LAPD. As part of her research for the film, McKinny met with Fuhrman twelve times, tape recording their conversations. In those meetings, Fuhrman revealed himself as a man who hated African Americans and was not shy about expressing his opinion on the subject. The conversations, filled with Fuhrman spouting racial epithets, filled about twelve hours of tape.

In July 1995 defense investigators got wind of the tapes and had Judge Ito subpoena them. If the jury could hear those tapes, the defense argued, they would learn firsthand what was in the mind of a police officer who was in a position to frame a famous black man for a double murder. In August, after listening to the tapes, Ito ruled that only two excerpts could be played for the jury. In the hushed courtroom, jurors heard two sentences in the voice of Mark Fuhrman: "We have no niggers where I grew up," and "That's where niggers live."[52] The jury did not hear the other thirty-nine times he had used the word, but they did not have to: Fuhrman, who said he had not used the word in the past ten years, was revealed as a liar.

Detective Mark Fuhrman's (seated) repeated denials of having used racial epithets had disastrous consequences for the prosecution's case.

On September 26 the jury had heard all the arguments from both sides, and it was time for closing arguments. Marcia Clark reviewed the evidence the prosecution had presented over the past eight months and tried to repair the damage done by Fuhrman's taped comments. In the end, she spoke for the two victims. "They both are telling you who did it—with their hair, their clothes, their bodies, their blood. They tell you he did it. He did it. Mr. Simpson. Orenthal Simpson. He did it."[53] When the defense's turn came, Johnnie Cochran summed up its case for the jury and spoke what was to become the most memorable line of the trial. Referring to the gloves that Simpson struggled to put on, Cochran said, "If it doesn't fit, you must acquit."[54]

With closing arguments over, Judge Ito instructed the jury to "conscientiously consider and weigh the evidence, apply the law and reach a just verdict, regardless of the consequences."[55] It was Friday, September 30, 1995. On Monday, October 2, the jury began deliberations that would determine whether O.J. Simpson would be a convicted murderer or a free man.

By the Numbers

100

The number of hairs taken from O.J. Simpson to compare with hairs found at the crime scene.

CHAPTER 5

Verdict and Repercussions

Shortly after 9:00 A.M. that Monday, the twelve members of the jury gathered in the deliberation room just behind Judge Ito's courtroom to decide O.J. Simpson's fate. The room was actually the same jury room that they had occupied for the last eight months during the times the jury was not needed in court. The jury foreperson was Armanda Cooley, a fifty-one-year-old African American resident of Los Angeles. Around the large table each juror sat in the same chair he or she had used during the trial. After a short discussion on how to conduct their deliberations, they took an initial poll to see where the jury members stood on Simpson's guilt or innocence. The poll revealed that ten jurors were for acquittal and two were for conviction. The members then began discussing the case, consulting several large folders containing pictures of the exhibits that had been presented in court. They raised questions about various pieces of evidence and talked about testimony they had heard over the course of the trial. Several questions about limousine driver Allan Park arose, so Cooley requested transcripts of his testimony. The judge arranged to have a court reporter read back Park's testimony from the official transcripts.

Marcia Clark had planned a shopping trip with a friend while the jury deliberated. When she heard about the jury's request for a read-back, she knew it could be either good or bad news. The Simpson jury wanted to review the testimony of one of the prosecution's best witnesses; if they believed Park's story, a guilty verdict was almost assured. Yet Clark was not ready to rejoice just yet, aware that even an experienced lawyer could not know the real reason for the request. Early Monday afternoon, Clark's cell phone rang. It was Christopher Darden, who gave her some surprising news. "The jury has a decision."[56] Clark was dumbfounded. Considering the mountain of evidence presented to the jury, she had expected deliberations to take a week or more. Yet now the jury on one of the most complex and highly publicized cases in legal history had made its decision in just a few short hours. Jeffrey Toobin, a journalist who covered the trial for *New Yorker* magazine, was also caught off guard by the decision. "No one—on either side or in the news media—had predicted so swift a verdict," he writes. "After all these months and all the debates over evidence, strategy, rulings, and rumors, only one question remained: What had the jurors done?"[57] Toobin, and everyone else, would find out when the verdict was read in court the next morning.

Judgment Day

Tuesday morning, October 3, was the final act in the media circus that had swirled around the eight-month duration of the O.J. Simpson murder trial. Los Angeles streets were cordoned off for blocks around the Criminal Courts Building. Hundreds of uniformed officers patrolled the area. Reporters and photographers thronged the halls as media helicopters buzzed overhead. According to Toobin, the television networks were prepared, even if somewhat excessively. "NBC had forty camera crews ready to roll for reaction to the verdict. ABC had assigned four producers to each juror."[58] Across the nation, everything seemed to halt as people gathered around their TVs and radios, waiting to hear the verdict.

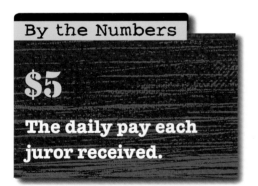

By the Numbers

$5

The daily pay each juror received.

Shortly before 10:00, Christopher Darden, Marcia Clark, and Johnnie Cochran entered the courtroom and took their places at their respective counsel tables. Then Simpson, wearing a gray suit and

yellow patterned tie, was escorted in and led to the defense table. When everyone was in place, the jury was brought in and,
with that, Judge Ito began the proceedings. "Mr. Simpson,
would you stand and face the jury?"[59] Simpson and his lawyers
stood, their faces a mixture of tension and hope. Then Dierdre
Robertson, Judge Ito's law clerk, read the first of the verdict
forms. "In the matter of the *People of the State of California vs.
Orenthal James Simpson*, we the jury, in the above titled action,
find the defendant, Orenthal James Simpson, not guilty of
the crime of murder in violation of penal code section 187a, a
felony, upon Nicole Brown Simpson."[60]

Simpson let out a sigh of relief and the tension instantly
seemed to leave his body. He managed a faint smile, then
waved and mouthed the words "thank you" to the jury. In

*Television crews,
satellite trucks, and
all the media circus
covering the Simpson
trial await a verdict
near the courthouse.*

Simpson, flanked by attorneys F. Lee Bailey (left) and Johnnie Cochran, reacts to the verdict of acquittal for double homicide.

the gallery, the Brown family sat stunned as Nicole's sisters began to cry. Robertson then read the second verdict form, announcing that Simpson was also not guilty of murdering Ron Goldman. Kim Goldman, Ron's sister, let out an anguished cry. The prosecution sat grimly and watched as the Dream Team patted Simpson on the back and congratulated each other. As the courtroom buzzed with mixed emotions of

both joy and disappointment, Ito proclaimed, "The defendant, having been acquitted of both charges, is ordered . . . released forthwith. All right. We'll stand in recess."[61]

The trial of the century was over. As the jury filed out of the courtroom, one juror, an African American male, turned toward the defense table and gave the "black power" salute—an upraised fist that silently spoke volumes.

Reasonable Doubt

At the beginning of the O.J. Simpson murder trial, some eight months before the not guilty verdicts were handed down, the prosecution was confident it had an almost airtight case against the former football star. Even in the absence of an eyewitness to the murders, Marcia Clark and her team felt that their forensic evidence, along with Simpson's history of domestic abuse against Nicole, was more than enough to win a conviction in court. As the events of October 3 ultimately showed, they could not have been more wrong. But how did the case go so badly off track?

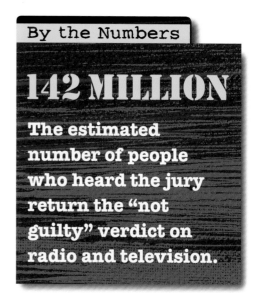

By the Numbers

142 MILLION

The estimated number of people who heard the jury return the "not guilty" verdict on radio and television.

In a criminal trial, the prosecution must prove to the jury that the defendant is guilty *beyond a reasonable doubt*. The prosecution does not have to prove one hundred percent conclusively that a person has committed a crime. A jury must simply be satisfied that, after reviewing the evidence, no reasonable person would doubt that the defendant is guilty. The Simpson jury felt that there was reasonable doubt. Armanda Cooley, the jury foreperson, explains:

> Based on the information that was presented, I felt that there was a lot of evidence that pointed to Mr. Simpson's guilt. . . . There were so many questions in my mind,

Homecoming

After his acquittal, O.J. Simpson wanted nothing more than to go home. Time *magazine describes Simpson's arrival at his estate:*

By 11:00 A.M. on October 3, O.J. Simpson was home, back at 360 North Rockingham, the mansion whose gates, landscaping and layout Americans have come to know so well. One of the first things the former football star saw was the silver-haired L.A. district attorney Gil Garcetti on TV, announcing that he had no plans to look for other killers. "Garcetti!" Simpson said aloud. "He wouldn't even give me that! Why doesn't that guy give me something—just say he'll look into it?" Simpson then retreated into his bedroom, sitting down on the edge of his huge bed and gazing at the space he hadn't seen in 474 days.

Simpson made some calls. He tried to reach "those guys from Brooklyn" —defense attorneys Barry Scheck and Peter Neufeld—who spent their first night of freedom enjoying another win: watching the Yankees beat the Seattle Mariners. He telephoned his former in-laws, the Browns, and made the case, yet again, for his innocence. When Simpson's mother Eunice settled into a chair, a friend said, "he just sat down beside her and looked into her eyes. No words."

Howard Chua-Eoan and Elizabeth Gleick, "Making the Case," *Time,* October 16, 1995. www.time.com/time/magazine/article/0,9171,983569-12,00.html.

however, and because we had no direct evidence and had to go on circumstantial evidence, I had no alternative at that time but to think he was not guilty. And it is important to remember that a not guilty verdict requires just one thing that can create reasonable doubt.[62]

The defense, said Simpson attorney Robert Shapiro, did just that. "Our job was to ask the questions, point out the improbables. For every single item—sock, glove, knit hat, blood— we were able to show doubt, reasonable and real."[63] Henry Lee, the defense forensic expert, commented that evidence can be useful only if it is handled properly. "Many authorities believe," Lee later wrote, "that physical evidence does not lie unless it has been contaminated, carelessly collected, mishandled, tampered with or planted. All these may apply to the Simpson case."[64]

Evidence in Question

While blood evidence was the keystone of the prosecution's case, the defense was able to discredit much of that evidence in the minds of the jury. Its basic argument was that Dennis Fung and Andrea Mazzola had botched the collection of blood samples, allowing them either to become contaminated with other samples of blood or to be physically degraded so that any tests performed on them would be suspect. For example, blood found on the back gate of the Bundy residence was not collected until three weeks after the murders. If it was simply missed in the initial investigation, it confirms the careless work done by the detectives and criminalists and leads to the possibility of natural degradation by the elements over time. If, however, it was not there at the time of the murders, it could have been planted by someone with the intent of framing Simpson for the murders. Either way, the evidence was of dubious quality. Even the testimony of the prosecution's expert witnesses turned out to be of little value in making its case. Even if, the jury might ask, the tests showed that it could only have been Simpson's blood at the crime scene, the tests were useless because the blood was contaminated.

In Simpson's bathroom at Rockingham, like most people's bathrooms, there was a clothes hamper. As Fung examined the scene on June 13, he took something out of the hamper to look at it. It was a dark pair of sweats, possibly the clothes that Kato Kaelin said Simpson was wearing the night of the murders. If anything might have forensic evidence on it, surely it would be a piece of clothing worn by a murderer during the commission of the crime. And yet Fung put the sweats back in the hamper instead of collecting them for evidence. "I figured if they'd been used in the murder," Fung explains, "the blood would be big and obvious. I didn't see any, so I put them back."[65] He apparently did not consider that if the killer were standing behind the victim, there might be only a little blood, not a large stain, on his clothing. And even a little blood could be tested. Fung, an experienced criminalist, had made a costly mistake.

The autopsy reports also proved problematic for the prosecution. Irwin Golden had performed the autopsies, and ordinarily he would have taken the witness stand for the prosecution. But Golden had been such a poor witness in the preliminary hearing that his supervisor, Lakshmanan Sathyavagiswaran, took the stand in his place. Sathyavagiswaran had the unfortunate job of explaining that Golden had made thirty errors in his autopsies of Nicole Simpson and Ron Goldman. Golden had labeled incorrectly some fluid from Simpson's body. He also had discarded Simpson's stomach contents, which, if kept, could have pinpointed more accurately her time of death. Sathyavagiswaran also contradicted Golden's contention that two knives (and thus two killers) could have been involved. He graphically demonstrated how a single assailant could have killed both victims in a short period of time.

But questionable forensic evidence alone did not lose the case for the prosecution. The defense had its own agenda that it pursued during the trial.

The Race Card

From the beginning, Simpson's defense team proposed the idea that the evidence that appeared so damaging to its case was planted by the Los Angeles Police Department, specifically criticizing the actions of detectives Mark Fuhrman and Philip Vannatter. Fuhrman had proved to be a racist. Why did he go to Rockingham on the night of the murders with Vannatter, Ronald Phillips, and Tom Lange? He was no longer on the case, and surely it did not take four detectives just to notify Simpson of his ex-wife's death. No, according to the defense, Fuhrman had with him the bloody right-hand glove he had secretly picked up at the Bundy crime scene. The defense speculated that Fuhrman first wiped the glove around the inside of the Bronco—depositing bloodstains on the steering wheel, seats, and console—and then dropped the glove behind Kaelin's room. And why did Vannatter carry around the vial of Simpson's blood instead of immediately booking it as evidence? Perhaps, the defense said, he used some of that blood to create the drops on the Rockingham driveway to implicate Simpson. Police also would have had to have planted blood on the rear gate at the Bundy residence and on the socks found in Simpson's bedroom. Such a plot to frame Simpson would have to involve at least several police officers or, at most, a grand conspiracy of officers, detectives, criminalists, technicians, coroner department personnel, and many others.

The defense left no detail to chance during the trial. For the jury's walk-through tour of the Rockingham estate, photographs

Becoming a Coroner

Job Description:
A coroner conducts inquiries into the cause of death to determine whether the death was due to natural causes, an accident, homicide, suicide, or the result of another cause. Coroners complete death certificates and testify in court concerning their findings.

Education:
A two- or four-year undergraduate degree in the life sciences is usually necessary (a medical examiner position requires a medical degree). Electives in such subjects as law, education, and government are helpful.

Qualifications:
Specific qualifications vary by location. Where coroners are elected, political experience is beneficial.

Salary:
Salaries vary greatly depending on the size of the employing municipality: ranges from $20,000 to more than $75,000.

Additional Information:
The ability to work on-call at all hours and to deal with bodies in various states of decomposition is necessary for a coroner. Good verbal and report writing skills are also required.

Criminalist Gary Sims points to bloodstains on Simpson's sock during the prosecution's case, which relied heavily on forensic evidence.

on the walls showing Simpson playing golf with rich white businessmen were taken down and replaced by pictures of African Americans. The prosecution also allowed race to enter the proceedings with a decision that some say lost them the case even before it began. Los Angeles County district attorney Gil Garcetti decided to have the case tried in downtown Los Angeles rather than in Santa Monica, the district where the murders took place. This location for the trial meant that the jury would most likely have a majority of African American members, reflecting the

racial makeup of the population of Los Angeles. Had the trial been held in Santa Monica, a largely white community, the jury most likely would have had a white majority. Garcetti explained that his decision was based on the fact that for a lengthy trial, as this one promised to be, the central location was more convenient for all concerned. In addition, it was a larger facility and better able to handle the sizable media contingency that was expected to be there on a daily basis. Perhaps the real reason, however, was that in 1992 Los Angeles had seen the worst riots in its history as a result of the acquittal of three white police officers charged with beating African American motorist Rodney King at a traffic stop. Garcetti did not want to see a similar incident occur in the wake of the Simpson trial. If Simpson were found guilty, perhaps the local community would more readily accept the verdict if it came from an African American jury. The fact that such a jury might be sympathetic to Simpson and find him not guilty did not seem to concern the prosecution; it felt that its forensic evidence was so overwhelming that any jury would have no choice but to render a guilty verdict.

After the trial, Shapiro stated, "Not only did we play the race card, we dealt it from the bottom of the deck."[66] According to Jeffrey Toobin, race plays a larger role in the American judicial system than most people realize: "For better or worse, American jurors have a long and still-flourishing tradition of both taking race into account in making their decisions, and denying that they are doing any such thing."[67] Public reaction to the not guilty verdict was divided along racial lines; whereas African Americans cheered when the verdict was announced, whites were stunned and silent. Yet many members of the jury claimed that race played no part in their deliberations. Jury foreperson Armanda Cooley writes,

> For all the time we were sequestered, we heard very little about racial stuff. I guess that's the reason why everybody on the jury, and I say everybody, was shocked when we learned racism was so heavily involved

Crowds outside the Criminal Courts Building in Los Angeles rejoice after hearing the not guilty verdict in the O.J. Simpson double homicide trial.

in people's reactions after the trial. . . . Jeanette Harris [a dismissed juror] summarized our predicament nicely when she said that race could have played a part in the verdict, but the evidence was so questionable that no one had to use the race card to come to a verdict.[68]

Ideally, a jury, whether white or African American, should look past the racial aspect of a case and deliver its verdict based on the quality of the evidence. But if race plays a greater role in American justice than we have admitted to ourselves, then we still have a long way to go to provide equal justice under the law for all.

Simpson's Next Trial

Although his murder trial was over, the legal system was not yet finished with O.J. Simpson. In a legal rule known as double jeopardy, being acquitted of the murder charges in the criminal trial prevents him from ever being tried for those crimes again. However, Simpson was eligible to be tried again under civil law, where individuals can sue other individuals for unlawful activity. In 1996 the Brown and Goldman families filed civil suits against Simpson for the wrongful death of Nicole and Ron and for survivorship claims. There were many differences between the civil and criminal trials. The civil trial was held not in Los Angeles, but in Santa Monica. The civil trial was not televised, and the jury was not sequestered. On the bench, Judge Hiroshi Fujisaki was a no-nonsense jurist who maintained control of the situation, keeping the court proceedings moving along in a way that Judge Ito had not.

Early on, Judge Fujisaki made an important ruling that turned the direction of the civil trial 180 degrees from the criminal trial. He declared that race would play no part in the civil proceedings because of the inflammatory effect it could have on the jury. This deprived the defense of one of the main weapons that was used so effectively by the Dream Team in the criminal trial. Another difference between the two trials was the way the law treats evidence in criminal versus civil cases. In a civil case, the prosecution must prove that the defendant is guilty by a preponderance of the evidence. This means that the evidence presented by the prosecution must be more convincing, or more probably true, in the minds of the jurors than the opposing evidence presented by the defense. This is a less stringent criterion than the reasonable doubt standard used in criminal trials. And rather than a unanimous verdict, only nine out of the twelve jurors have to agree.

O.J. Simpson Takes the Stand

The jury in the criminal trial did not get to hear Simpson's story from his own lips because the defense kept him from testifying. But in the civil trial, Simpson took the stand and underwent days of grueling direct examination by prosecutor Daniel Petrocelli. The following reveals Petrocelli challenging Simpson about his actions on the night of the murders.

Petrocelli: Nine thirty-five P.M. to 10:55 P.M., you cannot tell this jury the name of a single person—*living* person—that you saw or spoke to in that time. Is that correct?

Simpson: That is correct.

Petrocelli: And the reason why you didn't get in that Bronco [to go with Kato Kaelin to McDonald's] is because you used that Bronco to go to Nicole's condominium that evening after you came back from McDonalds. True?

Simpson: That's not true.

Petrocelli: You had gloves, you had a hat, you were wearing a dark sweat outfit, and you had a knife. And you went to Nicole Brown's condominium at 875 South Bundy, did you not, sir?

Simpson: That's absolutely not true!

Petrocelli: And you confronted Nicole Brown Simpson, and you killed her, didn't you?

Simpson: That's absolutely not true!

Petrocelli: And you killed Ronald Goldman, sir, did you or did you not?

Simpson: That's absolutely not true!

Quoted in Daniel Petrocelli with Peter Knobler, *Triumph of Justice: The Final Judgment on the Simpson Saga.* New York: Crown, 1998.

The civil trial began on October 23, 1996. Lead prosecutor Daniel Petrocelli presented the same forensic evidence that had been put forward in the criminal trial, but there were some important additions to the prosecution's evidence. The jury was shown thirty recently discovered photographs of Simpson wearing Bruno Magli shoes of the type that had made the bloody footprints at the Bundy crime scene. Petrocelli called many of the same witnesses to tell their stories to the new jury: Fung, Yamauchi, Park, Lee, Vannatter, and others appeared once more on the witness stand. There were, however, two notable changes in the witness lists: Detective Mark Fuhrman did not testify, but O.J. Simpson did. Simpson said that he never abused Nicole, and that he did not remember ever owning Bruno Magli shoes, despite the photographs presented in court. He testified that he could never murder his children's mother and leave her body where they could find it.

On January 28, 1997, the civil case against O.J. Simpson went to the jury. After sixteen hours of deliberation—compared to the criminal trial's deliberations of a mere four hours—the jury found Simpson liable for the deaths of Nicole Simpson and Ron Goldman. In addition, the jury awarded compensatory damages of $8.5 million. After another day of deliberation, it awarded an additional $25 million in punitive damages, making the total judgment against Simpson $33.5 million. Fred Goldman, Ron's father, said at the time, "We finally have justice for Ron and Nicole. Our family is grateful for a verdict of responsibility."[69]

Lessons from the Trials

If the O.J. Simpson murder trial proved anything, it is that nothing should be taken for granted when it comes to forensic evidence. Even the most incriminating evidence can be called into question if the collection, storage, and processing of that evidence are not done in the most professional manner. Police departments must make sure that their forensic personnel are using proper, strictly controlled scientific methods. Detectives and other crime scene personnel must be aware of the importance of evidence and take steps to avoid contamination. And prosecutors must realize that even the strongest circumstantial case can sometimes fail to persuade a jury.

After Simpson was acquitted in the criminal trial, he vowed to devote his life to finding the real killers of his ex-wife. In the years that followed, however, there was little indication that he would make good on that promise. He was often seen on the golf course, looking every bit like the Simpson America once knew and admired—waving, giving autographs, and flashing his winning smile. But behind that smile, only Simpson knows the truth of what happened on the night of June 12, 1994.

Notes

Introduction: O.J. and Nicole: Trouble in Paradise

1. Quoted in Sheila Weller, *Raging Heart: The Intimate Story of the Tragic Marriage of O.J. and Nicole Brown Simpson*. New York: Pocket, 1995, p. 125.

2. Quoted in Mark Cerasini, *O.J. Simpson: American Hero, American Tragedy*. New York: Pinnacle, 1994, pp. 297–98.

3. Quoted in Kenneth B. Noble, "Prosecution Says Simpson Abused Wife for 17 Years," *New York Times*, January 12, 1995. http://query.nytimes.com/gst/fullpage.html?res=990CE1DA123AF931A25752C0A963958260&sec=&spon=&pagewanted=print.

Chapter 1: Murder on Bundy Drive

4. Quoted in Jack Walraven, "Simpson Trial Transcripts," February 6, 1995. http://walraven.org/simpson/feb06.html.

5. Quoted in Henry C. Lee with Thomas W. O'Neill, *Cracking Cases: The Science of Solving Crimes*. Amherst, NY: Prometheus, 2002, p. 174.

6. Quoted in Lee with O'Neill, *Cracking Cases*, p. 175.

7. LeMoyne Snyder, *Homicide Investigation: Practical Information for Coroners, Police Officers, and Other Investigators*. Springfield, IL: Charles C. Thomas, 1977, p. 36.

8. Quoted in Tom Lange and Philip Vannatter as told to Dan E. Moldea, *Evidence Dismissed: The Inside Story of the Investigation of O.J. Simpson*. New York: Pocket, 1997, p. 10.

9. Quoted in Lange, Vannatter, and Moldea, *Evidence Dismissed*, p. 20.

10. Mark Fuhrman, *Murder in Brentwood*. Washington, DC: Regnery, 1997, p. 31.

11. Quoted in Marc Eliot, *Kato Kaelin: The Whole Truth*. New York: Harper Paperbacks, 1995, p. 95.

12. Fuhrman, *Murder in Brentwood*, p. 34.

13. Quoted in Lange, Vannatter, and Moldea, *Evidence Dismissed*, p. 31.

14. Quoted in Lange, Vannatter, and Moldea, *Evidence Dismissed*, p. 23.

15. Quoted in Jeffrey Toobin, *The Run of His Life: The People v. O.J. Simpson*. New York: Random House, 1996, p. 39.

16. Quoted in Toobin, *The Run of His Life*, p. 39.

17. Quoted in Toobin, *The Run of His Life*, p. 41.

Chapter 2: The Investigation

18. Quoted in *Famous American Trials*, "The O.J. Simpson Trial: Testimony of Dennis Fung," April 3, 1995. www. law.umkc.edu/faculty/projects/ftrials/ Simpson/fungtest.html.

19. Lange, Vannatter, and Moldea, *Evidence Dismissed*, p. 34.

20. Fuhrman, *Murder in Brentwood*, p. 39.

21. Fuhrman, *Murder in Brentwood*, p. 21.

22. Lange, Vannatter, and Moldea, *Evidence Dismissed*, p. 75.

23. Lange, Vannatter, and Moldea, *Evidence Dismissed*, p. 95.

24. Lange, Vannatter, and Moldea, *Evidence Dismissed*, p. 99.

Chapter 3: Examining the Evidence

25. Marcia Clark with Theresa Carpenter, *Without a Doubt*. New York: Viking, 1997, p. 68.

26. Quoted in Walraven, "Simpson Trial Transcripts," May, 24, 1995. http://wal raven.org/simpson/may24.html.

27. Clark with Carpenter, *Without a Doubt*, p. 32.

28. Clark with Carpenter, *Without a Doubt*, p. 32.

29. Lange, Vannatter, and Moldea, *Evidence Dismissed*, p. 148.

30. Quoted in Lawrence Schiller and James Willwerth, *American Tragedy: The Uncensored Story of the Simpson Defense*. New York: Random House, 1996, p. 50.

31. Quoted in Schiller and Willwerth, *American Tragedy*, p. 50.

32. Quoted in Lange, Vannatter, and Moldea, *Evidence Dismissed*, p. 154.

33. Quoted in Toobin, *The Run of His Life*, p. 91.

34. Quoted in Toobin, *The Run of His Life*, p. 105.

35. Quoted in Toobin, *The Run of His Life*, p. 107.

36. Quoted in Lange, Vannatter, and Moldea, *Evidence Dismissed*, p. 168.

37. Quoted in Toobin, *The Run of His Life*, p. 110.

Chapter 4: The Trial of the Century

38. Quoted in B. Drummond Ayres Jr., "The Simpson Case: The Overview; Simpson Ordered to Stand Trial in Slaying of Ex-Wife and Friend," *New York Times*, July 9, 1994. http://query. nytimes.com/gst/fullpage.html?res= 9404E0DB173FF93AA35754 C0A962958260.

39. Quoted in Clark with Carpenter, *Without a Doubt*, p. 125.

40. Christopher Darden with Jess Walter, *In Contempt*. New York: Regan, 1996, pp. 166, 167.

41. Darden with Walter, *In Contempt*, pp. 221–22.

42. Quoted in Darden with Walter, *In Contempt*, p. 222.

43. Quoted in Jack Walraven, "The Simpson Trial Transcripts," January 25, 1995. http://walraven.org/simpson/jan25.html.

44. Quoted in Toobin, *The Run of His Life*, p. 320.

45. Quoted in Walraven, "Simpson Trial Transcripts," March 21, 1995. http://walraven.org/simpson/mar21.html.

46. Quoted in Frontline, "The O.J. Verdict: Interviews: Gerald Uelmen." www.pbs.org/wgbh/pages/frontline/oj/interviews/uelmen.html.

47. Clark with Carpenter, *Without a Doubt*, p. 395.

48. Quoted in O.J. Simpson Trial Transcript, May 11, 1995.

49. Quoted in Walraven, "Simpson Trial Transcripts," June 15, 1995. http://walraven.org/simpson/jun15.html.

50. Quoted in David Margolick, "Victims Put Up Long Fight, a Witness for Simpson Says," *New York Times*, August 11, 1995. http://query.nytimes.com/gst/fullpage.html?res=990CE3D9163CF932A2575BC0A963958260&scp=99&sq=august+11%2C+1995.

51. Quoted in Robert L. Shapiro, *The Search for Justice—a Defense Attorney's Brief on the O.J. Simpson Case*. New York: Warner, 1996, p. 325.

52. Quoted in Toobin, *The Run of His Life*, p. 407.

53. Clark with Carpenter, *Without a Doubt*, p. 474.

54. *Famous American Trials*, "The O.J. Simpson Trial: Closing Argument of Johnnie Cochran (Excerpts)." www.law.umkc.edu/faculty/projects/ftrials/Simpson/cochranclose.html.

55. Quoted in 'Lectric Law Library, "Judge Ito's 9/95 Instructions in O.J.'s Criminal Case." www.lectlaw.com/files/cas62.htm.

Chapter 5: Verdict and Repercussions

56. Quoted in Clark with Carpenter, *Without a Doubt*, p. 476.

57. Toobin, *The Run of His Life*, p. 428.

58. Toobin, *The Run of His Life*, p. 429.

59. Quoted in Armanda Cooley, Carrie Bess, and Marsha Rubin-Jackson, *Madam Foreman: A Rush to Judgment?* Beverly Hills, CA: Dove, 1995, p. 2.

60. Quoted in Cooley, Bess, and Rubin-Jackson, *Madam Foreman*, p. 2.

61. Quoted in Toobin, *The Run of His Life*, p. 431.

62. Cooley, Bess, and Rubin-Jackson, *Madam Foreman*, p. 194.

63. Shapiro, *The Search for Justice*, p. 278.

64. Henry Lee and Jerry Labriola, *Famous Crimes Revisited: From Sacco-Vanzetti to O.J. Simpson*. Southington, CT: Strong, 2001, p. 240.

65. Quoted in Clark with Carpenter, *Without a Doubt*, p. 377.

66. Quoted in Toobin, *The Run of His Life*, p. 438.

67. Toobin, *The Run of His Life*, p. 437.

68. Cooley, Bess, and Rubin-Jackson, *Madam Foreman*, p. 182.

69. Quoted in Crime Library, "Justice for the Dead." www.crimelibrary.com/notorious_murders/famous/simpson/dead_16.html.

For More Information

Books

Marc Cerasini, *O.J. Simpson: American Hero, American Tragedy*. New York: Pinnacle, 1994. A popular biography of O.J. Simpson from his early life through his slow-speed car chase and arrest. Includes a transcript of Nicole Simpson's 911 phone call.

Mark Fuhrman, *Murder in Brentwood*. Washington, DC: Regnery, 1997. The controversial LAPD detective tells his side of the investigation, refuting the defense's contention that he planted evidence to frame Simpson.

Tom Lange and Philip Vannatter with Dan E. Moldea, *Evidence Dismissed: The Inside Story of the Police Investigation of O.J. Simpson*. New York: Pocket, 1997. Detectives Lange and Vannatter meticulously detail the police investigation from its beginning at the Bundy crime scene to Simpson's acquittal.

Henry C. Lee with Thomas W. O'Neill, *Cracking Cases: The Science of Solving Crimes*. Amherst, NY: Prometheus, 2002. The forensic investigation of Ron Goldman's and Nicole Simpson's murders as told by the defense's star witness. Includes several chapters on other cases Lee investigated.

Katherine Ramsland, *The C.S.I. Effect*. New York: Berkley Boulevard, 2006. The author discusses the latest forensic techniques as portrayed by the popular television show and revisits the Simpson case and others where forensics has played a major role.

Sheila Weller, *Raging Heart: The Intimate Story of the Tragic Marriage of O.J. and Nicole Brown Simpson*. New York: Pocket, 1995. This story of their troubled relationship includes details of O.J.'s abuse of Nicole and her attempts to repair their broken marriage. Includes many family snapshots.

Web Sites

CNN, "O. J. Simpson Main Page" (www.cnn.com/US/OJ). The Web site offers the Cable News Network's coverage of the Simpson case. It includes short biographies, timelines, photographs, and animations.

Crime Library, "The O. J. Simpson Murder Trial" (www.crimelibrary.com/notorious_murders/famous/simpson/index_1.html). An in-depth look at the murders, the trial, and the aftermath. It includes a review of the 2007 book by O.J. Simpson, *If I Did It*.

Famous American Trials, "The O.J. Simpson Trial" (www.law.umkc.edu/faculty/projects/ftrials/Simpson/simpson.htm). A university law professor's site that analyzes the Simpson case in detail. It includes an examination of the evidence and excerpts from the trial transcripts.

How Stuff Works, "How Crime Scene Investigation Works" (http://science.howstuffworks.com/csi.htm). A complete guide to the investigation of crime scenes, with links to eight subsequent chapters.

Human Genome Project Information, "DNA Forensics" (www.ornl.gov/sci/techresources/Human_Genome/elsi/forensics.shtml). This site presents the basics of DNA identification and analysis. It contains numerous links to examples of forensic DNA use and other relevant Web sites.

Wagner and Son, "The O. J. Simpson Case" (www.wagnerandson.com/oj/OJ.htm). An interesting site that presents one man's speculation of how Nicole Simpson and Ron Goldman were murdered, not by O.J. Simpson, but by two mob hit men. It contains many interesting photos and diagrams.

Index

Picture Credits

About the Author

Craig E. Blohm has written numerous magazine articles on historical subjects for children for more than twenty years, and he has authored many books for Lucent Books. He has written for social studies textbooks and has conducted workshops in writing history for children. A native of Chicago, Blohm and his wife, Desiree, live in Tinley Park, Illinois, and have two sons, Eric and Jason.